WILLIE SULLIVAN is the Director of Elector: a political campaigner, activist and suppo: many areas of public life. He has worked _. _____ voluntary and public sector. He was the Campaign consultant on the successful Fairshare Campaign for the introduction of STV for Scottish local government and was Campaign Director for Vote for a Change, the campaign to secure a referendum on electoral reform. Willie is also involved at a Scottish and UK level in Compass, and has written widely on politics, participation and ideas. This is his first book.

Open Scotland is a series which aims to open up debate about the future of Scotland and do this by challenging the closed nature of many conversations, assumptions and parts of society. It is based on the belief that the closed Scotland has to be understood, and that this is a prerequisite for the kind of debate and change society needs to have to challenge the status quo. It does this in a non-partisan, pluralist and open-minded manner, which contributes to making the idea of self-government into a genuine discussion about the prospects and possibilities of social change.

Luath Press is an independently owned and managed book publishing company based in Scotland, and is not aligned to any political party or grouping. *Viewpoints* is an occasional series exploring issues of current and future relevance.

The Missing Scotland

Why over a million Scots choose not to vote
and what it means for our democracy

WILLIE SULLIVAN

in association with the Electoral Reform Society

☐Electoral
☐Reform
☐Society
  Scotland

Luath Press Limited
EDINBURGH
www.luath.co.uk

First published 2014

ISBN: 978-1-910021-39-2

The paper used in this book is recyclable. It is made from
low chlorine pulps produced in a low energy, low emissions manner
from renewable forests.

Typeset in 11 point Sabon
by 3btype.com

Contents

Acknowledgements

Thanks to go to Gavin, Jennie, Senga, Thomas, Louise, Rosie and Danielle and the fantastic team at Luath Press...

Ideas never really belong to one person. They are the result of reading, talking, watching, listening and sharing with other people. I would like to thank Gerry Hassan for asking me to write this book and for the many fascinating and enlightening conversations we have where many ideas are developed.

In the same light I would like to thank Neal Lawson and everyone else that makes Compass such a stimulating and supportive organisation to be part of.

For the in depth focus group research that is the foundation of this book I would like to thank IPSOS MORI Scotland and in particular Mark Diffley, Sara Davidson and Ciaran Mulholland.

For their support, contributions, and encouragement I would like to thanks my colleagues and friends at the Electoral Reform Society: Katie Ghose, Kate West, Darren Hughes, Juliet Swann, Will Brett, Jessica Garland, Chris Terry, Stuart Thomas, Stephen Brooks, Owain ap Gareth, Sarah Allan, Davina Johnston and all the Council members.

I also thank Paul Cairney, Michael Keating and A. Wilson for their permission to use their unpublished research on MSPs' backgrounds.

And I gratefully acknowledge the contributions made to this book though research, writing and conversations by Oliver Escobar, John Curtice, Robin McAlpine, Martin Stephens, Ashley De, David Runciman and Lawrence Freedman.

CHAPTER ONE

We Are All Democrats Now!

IT IS 9 MARCH 2014. Posters on polling stations flap in the breeze. Balloons and bunting give a muted tone of celebration. Small queues form as people line up to cast their vote. The media are reporting an excited electorate and a very high turnout. It is Election Day in Mount Paekdu district – the constituency of current North Korean leader, Kim Jong-un.

Across the country, North Koreans come out to vote for their representatives to the Supreme People's Assembly, as they do every five years. On each ballot paper there is one name only and the voters have a simple choice of Yes or No. It is not known if anyone has ever voted No. Certainly in Kim Jong-un's constituency, the state media reported that not a single vote was cast against the incumbent – and that on a 100 per cent turnout. It would not be viewed as a democratic act to vote against Kim Jong-un, rather one of extreme foolhardiness, or else treason. We can only imagine what would be the painful outcome for any voter that dared to dissent.

North Korea is probably the least democratic country in the world, but one that goes out of its way to name itself a democracy and to still hold elections for its Supreme People's Assembly (*Economist Explains*, 2014). It is strange and fascinating that even the world's most despotic leaders spend considerable amounts of money on running elections. They are of course a sham, an attempt to give some form of legitimacy to their regimes, but that they should go to such an effort says a lot about the universal power of the idea of 'democracy,' best captured long ago in Abraham Lincoln's statement: 'government of the people by the people for people'. Now, with Burma's transition into pseudo-democracy, the only countries in the world that do not feel it necessary to claim that they are democracies are Saudi Arabia and Vatican City.

In Scotland we live in what we think is a democracy, but as the Democratic Republic of Korea demonstrates, naming it is a long way from realising it. Most places claim to be democracies. The list of United Nation member states includes countries claiming it in their title, including The Democratic Republic of Congo and the Lao People Democratic Republic, but neither is a shining light of democratic practice.

Scotland, the UK and the EU (we have several levels of government) are of course far removed from these pretend 'democratic republics.' Looking at these places should make us grateful that we live in a state that operates arguably an advanced level of democracy. Here we have many freedoms, the rule of law, and our rights are enshrined and protected in traditions and conventions and, more recently, through the Human Rights Act. However, gratitude at not being the worst should not translate into an acceptance of not being as good as we could be. Once it has taken root, democracy is tenacious and adaptive, but it is not inevitable that it either stays or progresses. Democratic freedoms can go down as well as up.

The Economist Intelligence Unit Democracy Index 2013 states:

> Free and fair elections and civil liberties are necessary conditions for democracy, but they are unlikely to be sufficient for a full and consolidated democracy if unaccompanied by transparent and at least minimally efficient government, sufficient political participation and a supportive democratic political culture. It is not easy to build a sturdy democracy. Even in long-established ones, democracy can corrode if not nurtured and protected.

This book seeks to examine three questions by looking at the people who are currently missing from our democracy in Scotland, that being those who are excluded and/or have opted out of direct engagement.

The first question that will be posed is whether Scotland is as democratic as we think it is. The second concerns how safe our democracy is and whether our rights and freedoms are threatened by the fact that large parts of our population are missing from the actual operation of our democracy. The third will think about how we can bring those that are missing back, to reinvigorate democracy perhaps in an evolved form and in doing so, bring our country closer together.

Why is democracy important?

We need to believe that democracy works in Scotland. We have to think that the government who controls and directs the civil service, the public services and the other parts of the state of Scotland is acting in the interests of the public. We must believe that it will do so because it is in its interests and because its members are part of the people, but also because they have our power on loan. If they do not act on our behalf then we, the people, can remove their power and vote them out at the next election.

While the state ultimately has the power to make us obey laws, things work much better if people feel that they do not want to break laws, and as citizens operate a level of obligation to the good of the wider society by paying taxes and generally supporting the running of the state. This is true even in North Korea, where rules are enforced with a violently nasty apparatus – those who enact it have an easier job if people believe that it is for the wider good. In Scotland we require a level of consensus and agreement and cooperation with the state. This public consensus, the views of our families and friends, probably affects how much we conform to the agreed rules of our society more than threats of fines or other punishments from the state.

The ability to force people to do things and to punish them if they do not must retain broad support for it to work. Public services and activities should be carried out with people's support, but focussing for a moment on the coercive functions of the state helps to understand the essential nature of this support. Policing, courts, fines and prisons should be there by tolerance and consent and controlled by the rule of laws made by democratic legislators. Without popular consent, these actions would be oppressive, as they are in states where the population has little real power and are forced from above to acquiesce. Political scientists and philosophers term the proper acceptance of authority 'legitimacy' – Scotland's body politic has legitimacy, whereas North Korea's does not.

There are long-running ideological clashes about how this legitimacy originates and indeed what it actually is. Great political thinkers including Rawls, Hume, Rousseau, Mill, Kant and many others have explored these ideas of authority and legitimacy – concepts contested because they are so very basic to how any country is run. Ensuring all authority is genuinely legitimate would allow human beings to be as free as possible from oppression and as free as possible to create a good society. An illegitimate state is by definition an oppressive state.

Extreme cases such as North Korea show blatantly that the powerful will often seek sham legitimacy. While this manufactured legitimacy is obvious in such places, it exists to some level here as well. The government and other institutions of power often run consultations and listening exercises that are not really democratic, and claim or imply that they are. In the lead up to the 'Edinburgh Agreement' between Holyrood and Westminster, which set the terms for Scottish referendum on independence, both Governments held public consultations which requested evidence being submitted to an email address. Unsurprisingly, only a small number of highly motivated and interested individuals and organisations took part, making politicians later claims, such as '75 per cent of the responders wanted a single question' virtually meaningless in terms of democratic authority (Black 2012) and deliberately misleading.

Philosophers have argued for centuries about whether consent is necessary for legitimacy, and indeed whether democracy is necessary for legitimacy (in Saudi Arabia and Vatican City it would seem that legitimacy conferred by a divinity remains sufficient, as it was here for a long time). This might all be cerebral fun for academics and philosophers, but it is important to connect with what is happening now in Scotland. The simple test would seem to be whether Scots would accept a government that they did not think had won a fair election. We would hope that only a public perception of a party winning a democratic election could give a government permission to govern.

It could be said that legitimacy was briefly questioned in the 2007 Scottish Parliament elections. An unusually large number of votes, representing 2.9 per cent of all those cast on the constituency ballot and 4.1 per cent on the list, were deemed invalid (Gould 2007). This resulted in considerable media furore and widespread public disquiet, but despite serious concerns in some quarters, the parties felt it better to accept the results and steady the system rather than challenge the election. This seems to demonstrate that many Scots need to believe our democracy is working for it to be secure and stable, yet more and more of the population opt out of the most fundamental expression of faith and trust in that democratic process: voting in an election.

Mapping 'the Missing Scotland'

There are around four million people registered to vote in Scotland and another estimated 400,000–500,000 eligible but not registered, prior to the referedum drive. Compared to other similar states, ten per cent plus of unregistered voters is low to average (Terry 2012). The United States of America, for example, has only 68 per cent, while at the other end of the scale Canada, Australia, and New Zealand are all in the low 90s. These high rates of registration are partly because these countries have compulsory registration and the ability to register on voting day itself. There is now a danger that our registration rate will fall further. UK legislation that used to require the head of household to register everyone in the house and face a fine if they did not return the information was changed so that each individual is responsible. This was the biggest change to registration since the universal franchise was adopted in 1928, and time is now tight for local authority electoral registration officers to achieve the planned implementation (tying in with the Scottish referendum and the UK General Election).

Having over ten per cent of the electorate not even registered to cast their vote cannot be satisfactory. It is possible to speculate at why these people are not registered to vote. Many will be young people who may see little point in voting and/or are moving frequently. Some will be trying to escape from debt or feel uncomfortable about being on a register that identifies them and their address. Many people will just have not got around to it and many will see no point in registering as they do not want to vote. If we are to convince more of these people to take part in our democracy, the reasons for registering to vote must outweigh the reasons not to.

The turnout in the 2011 Scottish Elections was just over 50 per cent, which means that nearly two million Scots who could vote, did not. Even with the higher General Election turnout of 63.8 per cent in 2010, that leaves 1.5 million people that did not vote. The term 'the missing Scotland' has been used during the Scottish referendum debate by commentators and others to refer to those Scottish citizens and voters who a generation ago voted and took part in elections but no longer do so, but may come out and vote in the referendum. Figures from Electoral Commission Scotland reveal that 989,540 voters are missing from the 2011 Scottish Parliament elections if adjusted for the 75 per cent turnout of the 1992 UK General Election in Scotland (Hassan, 2014). This has made them a vital target group for the two campaigns, whereas in all other elections they have largely been ignored. The fact that this number of people may have made an active choice not to vote distorts our politics and may represent a serious threat to our democracy.

Over the last century, an ideal of a nation state has developed containing several elements including rule of law, human rights and freedoms as well as elected governments. This ideal seems to respect the principle that all citizens are of equal value, at least politically. Debates raged around suffrage for centuries. Eventually all men got the vote, and then all woman, and now – in the year of the referendum on Scottish independence – all people over the age of 16. It does no harm to remember that just 100 years ago, only landowners could vote, and there are woman alive today who voted in the first election in which woman could do so. In other words, what was thought to be the realisation of this ideal of liberal democracy is still relatively young. For some it was thought to be the zenith of human civilisation that Francis Fukuyama famously and foolishly called 'the end of history' (Fukuyama 1989), by which he implied that the principles of liberal democracy may have been the ideal that could not be bettered. Freedom, Equality and Democracy – history still has a long way to run in increasing, spreading and protecting these principles.

While this is not the end of history, much has been achieved. The burning question is: if after centuries of struggle to reach this ideal, an ideal that most still support and aspire to, why did only 50.4 per cent of Scots vote in the 2011 Scottish Parliament elections (Curtice and Steven 2011) and only 39.5 per cent in the 2012 local government elections (Curtice 2012)?

It could be that people are quite happy with how things are and do not feel the need to change anything, but a range of survey data does not support this. In the 2011 Scottish Attitudes Survey, just 18 per cent of Scots trusted the UK Government to act in Scotland's best interests and only 24 per cent of those over 15 years of age across the UK tended to trust the Government (Office for National Statistics 2014). Voter turnout in UK General Elections peaked in 1950 with over eight in ten (82 per cent) of the electorate voting, in 2010 the turnout was 61 per cent. The Hansard Society's annual democracy audit has shown a steady decline in trust and perceived effectiveness of politics over the ten years it has been conducted (Korris 2013).

A large number of people have stopped participating in the political and democratic process for reasons other than that they are content. Most worryingly of all, this is a growing situation amongst the young. The purpose of this book is to discover more about these people. Who are they? Why do they not take part? What are their concerns? Would politics and Scotland be different if they joined in? And perhaps most importantly, what would have to change to make that a possibility?

CHAPTER TWO

The Non-Voters

Who doesn't vote and political inequality

Table 1 – Scottish Council Elections 2012 – Four Lowest Turnout Wards, then lowest by City

Overall Position by Turnout numbered Lowest to Highest	Turnout as per cent registered to vote	Ward Name	Council
1 (lowest)	20.46	George St Harbour	Aberdeen
2	21.96	Tillydrone-Seaton-Old Aberdeen	Aberdeen
3	23.6	Anderston City	Glasgow
4	26.3	Calton	Glasgow
10	29.72	Maryfield	Dundee
41	34.56	Gorgie Sighthill	Edinburgh

Source: Electoral Reform Society Data

Table 2 – Scottish Council Elections 2012 – Four Highest Turnout Wards, then highest by City

Overall Position by Turnout numbered Lowest to Highest	Turnout as per cent registered to vote	Ward Name	Council
353 (highest)	63.86	Shetland West	Shetland
352	61.14	North Isle	Shetland
351	61.09	Sgire-An-Rubha	Western Isles

Overall Position by Turnout numbered Lowest to Highest	Turnout as per cent registered to vote	Ward Name	Council
350	60.58	Sgir'-Uige-Agus-Ceann-A-Tuath-Nan-Loch	Westen Isles
311	47.85	Inverlieth	Edinburgh
314	48.8	The Ferry	Dundee
245	43.75	Lower Deeside	Aberdeen
226	42.74	Pollokshields	Glasgow

Source: Electoral Reform Society Data

Survey data from the likes of the Hansard Society Annual Audit consistently shows that people that belong to social groups with manual labour jobs or unemployed (social class D and E) are much less likely to vote than managerial and professional workers (social class A and B). Election turnout in the 2012 Scottish Local Government elections by ward seems to confirm the relationship between social class and turnout. Wards with high levels of deprivation and high student populations tend to have the lowest turnouts, while Island communities and/or relatively affluent areas tend to have much higher turnouts.

In the 2011 Scottish Parliament elections, turnout varied considerably between those constituencies with well-off populations and those with high levels of poverty. One clear indicator of this difference is how turnout varies according to the proportion of people who in answering the 2001 Census indicated that they were in good health. As Table 3 shows, turnout was on average nearly ten points higher in constituencies in which a large proportion said they were in good health than it was in those with poorer health. This gap seems, if anything, to have widened further since 2007. This happened in part because, contrary to the nationwide trend, constituency turnout actually increased in the (relatively affluent) Lothian's electoral region centred on Edinburgh. This social variation in the level of turnout is also clearly illustrated by those seats that lie at the top and the bottom of the league table of constituency turnouts shown in Table 4. The highest turnout was in Eastwood (63.2 per cent), a highly affluent suburb to the south of Glasgow, while two middle-class Edinburgh seats, Southern (61.6 per cent) and Western (59.4 per cent), are also amongst the top four. The lowest turnout was recorded in a seat in the east end of Glasgow, Glasgow Provan (34.8 per cent), while no constituencies in the city occur above the bottom seven places in the table (Curtice 2012).

Table 3 – Average turnout in constituency grouped
by reported levels of good health

Percent in Good Health Since 2007	Turnout	Change per cent
0–67	45.5	-1.8 (24)
67–71	51.9	-1.5 (33)
71+	55.1	-0.5 (16)

Main cell entries are means.
Figures in brackets show the number of constituencies that fall into that category.
Data on person per cent in good health are taken from the 2001 Census.

Table 4 – Highest and lowest turnout by constituency
(on the Constituency Vote), 2011

Highest Turnout	Per cent	Lowest Turnout	Per cent
Eastwood	63.2 per cent	Glasgow Provan	34.8 per cent
Edinburgh Southern	61.6 per cent	Glasgow Maryhill and Springburn	36.3 per cent
Na h-Eileanan an Iar	59.6 per cent	Glasgow Shettleston	37.9 per cent
Edinburgh Western	59.4 per cent	Glasgow Pollok	39.2 per cent
Stirling	58.3 per cent	Glasgow Kelvin	39.7 per cent
East Lothian	57.1 per cent	Glasgow Anniesland	43.2 per cent
Edinburgh Pentlands	57.1 per cent	Glasgow Southside	43.2 per cent
Strathkelvin and Bearsden	56.9 per cent	Cunninghame South	43.3 per cent
Perthshire North	56.1 per cent	Aberdeen Central	43.9 per cent

Source: Electoral Reform Society

Young People

Many of the lowest turnout wards shown in the tables are city centre areas with high student populations. It is not surprising that students are unlikely to vote. First of all, they are largely transient, and less linked to issues that affect their local community, with their time there relatively short. This is in sharp contrast to island communities, who vote in local elections in numbers that would be high for a general election in any part of the Scottish mainland. Islanders tend to have strong connections to place and to the community of that place. Crofters new and old have a settled connection with the land, with family ties, or have chosen to live there because of the nature of island life. Students are also predominantly young, and young people are less likely to vote. This is getting less likely with each generation. The Hansard Society's 2013 annual audit of political engagement in the UK found a marked decrease in the proportion of 18–24 year olds who are certain to vote (from 22 per cent in 2012 to 12 per cent in 2013); the same survey identified that more than four times as many people aged 55 and above are certain to vote than 18–24 year olds (Korris 2013). It is a common misconception that political disinterest is part of being young and that the young, with few responsibilities, are focused on other priorities. Of course these factors probably have an effect, but previous generations of young people have certainly voted in much greater numbers, and surveys such as Hansard indicate that engagement with formal politics from this age group is in rapid decline.

Finding out more about non-voters

To understand more fully the reasons why the young and the disadvantaged are not voting, it is best to ask them. In Dec 2013/Jan 2014, IPSOS Mori conducted three focus groups for this book: two held in Glasgow, recruited mainly from Anderston City Ward, and one in Dundee. One of the Glasgow groups comprised young people under the age of 25 (hereafter referred to as the 'young group') and the other two groups were across all age groups (Dundee Group and Glasgow Group). All groups were made up of people who would not vote in an immediate election; some may have voted in the past but they did not vote anymore. Participants were not selected by their social class but for not voting, so most were from social class D/E (semi-skilled/non-skilled manual labour/non-working). The next section summarises the focus group findings, with some text taken directly from the IPSOS Mori report.

What non-voters care about

One key point, true of all participants, is that they are not apathetic about where they live, or about the desire for it to be better. Any suggestion that non-voters are uninterested and broadly disengaged beyond voting was not borne out by this research. When asked to talk about politics, particpants addressed it often through the frames and language provided by political parties and the mass media, but in a very personal way. They could easily identify the problems within their communities and the circumstances that, if changed, would make them better places to live. These problems included unemployment, bad housing or homelessness, addictions and lack of facilities. They were concerned about their future, and the future of their family and friends and the people they know. While many had jobs, they were worried about losing them. They did not view people on benefits as scroungers but as people they had relationships with, as potentially their friends and their family. Participants saw benefits cuts, and particularly the 'bedroom tax' (which had a high media profile at the time of the research), as adversely affecting people they knew. They felt that they could easily be in the position of 'worklessness' or even homelessness.

All the groups were asked to come up with potential actions or methods that they might employ to address some of the problems they identified in their areas. Unsurprisingly, voting did not arise spontaneously from the conversation but was arrived at eventually in the two general groups. All of the suggested methods involved pressurising the authorities or the state to do 'something about it' and self-organisation, or action was not raised. The perceived relative effectiveness of the methods brought up in discussion varied between the groups. The general public group felt that the most effective method would be writing to a politician and protesting, while the least effective would be voting. The young group felt that the most effective methods would be petitioning and developing a social media campaign, and the least effective would be contacting a politician (there was no mention of voting in this group). Participants in the Dundee group did not feel that any of the methods were particularly effective, linking this to a sense that people do not have the confidence or knowledge to successfully use these methods (particularly contacting politicians and petitioning). In this group, voting was considered ineffective, as it is 'voiceless': 'You are voting to agree with a party's policies, not get your own voice across.'

This is a very telling statement. It hints at an agenda set by others that is different from theirs, and was a theme that came up several times in the groups. Participants recognised that they have a choice in voting, but options arising through voting are set by others who are unlike them, and none of those options are felt to make much sense.

Why they don't vote

All group members had very little regard for politicians or for voting. The participants who had voted in past elections said that they had done so because their family had always voted or because 'it's just what you did'. They often went on to say that they had invariably voted for candidates that their parents had favoured, it was a family tradition, and that 'policy didn't come into it':

> It had nothing to do with what [the parties] had to offer; I think we all know that's a lot of crap.
>
> General public group, Glasgow

At the same time, participants often discussed their past voting behaviour in terms of their predominantly working-class backgrounds. Indeed, one participant stated explicitly that when he was younger, voting was 'a working-class thing'. Another contended that more people voted in the past because households used to be more 'political', owing to the influence of trade unions in society.

In terms of other reasons given for voting in past elections, a few participants commented that politicians used to be more trustworthy and were therefore more deserving of their vote. Another commented that voting used to make him 'feel part of something', as the media would present elections as important national events. One participant in Dundee stated that people are inclined to vote during periods when a particular party or campaign has popularity, and that some people would generally 'go with the flow'.

In all groups, the main reasons given for not voting in past elections were:

- 'There's no left or right anymore… naebody's prepared to stick their neck out.' In other words, there is no perceived difference between parties and their objectives.

- A view that 'No-one represents my interests.'

- 'It's just like a playground fight between the big boys.' (Dundee group) A lack of trust in politicians and an elite that are not like the voters.

- A perception that manifesto commitments are rarely followed through on: 'They say one thing and do another.' (young group, Glasgow).

- A feeling that voting is unlikely to make a difference and is therefore a waste of time.

- A lack of (concise) information about how to go about voting, who the candidates are and what they stand for, and a lack of real choice between candidates.

Additionally, participants in the younger group said that they had not voted in the past because they felt that doing so would make little difference to the issues that mattered most to them. That is, that politicians and parties did not do enough to oppose the 'bedroom tax,' to tackle unemployment among young people, or to do anything to make housing rents more affordable. A couple also contended that politics was too 'London dominated' and their votes would simply be wasted. For some of the young group, voting was treated almost with disdain: if you voted then you were being manipulated. 'Do you think I'm zipped up the back?' was a response from one member of this group when asked about voting. 'I'm no giving any of *them* my vote' also implied a sense that their vote was valuable and important, but none of the options on offer were worthy of it. Significantly, participants tended not to discriminate between different types of election when discussing their reasons for not voting. This reflected a deep level of distrust in politicians, as well as participants' general lack of confidence that their vote would make a difference.

Some people did raise issues that are practical barriers to voting. These include:

- A lack of knowledge about the issues
- A lack of knowledge about how to register for vote
- A lack of choice – no online voting available
- Being too busy, especially if you have a job and a family

The majority of participants were, however, clear that these more practical issues were less important in dissuading them from voting than fundamental issues about parties and politicians. In fact, several where adamant that it was not about how easy it was to vote, but about there being no-one that they would want to vote for. The 'young group' were particularly clear that regardless of whether they could vote online, or via their mobile phone, reducing some barriers, if nothing else changed they would still not vote.

What might make people vote in future elections?

The overriding point emerging from this part of the discussion in the focus groups was that for the vast majority of participants, not voting in elections was a deliberate act. They claimed to want to vote but were so disillusioned with the political process that they had opted out. Participants talked about a range of issues that could make them change their minds and (re)engage with the political process; this included having more honest, trustworthy and better quality politicians (explored below), politicians fulfilling manifesto promises and having a wider range of choice among political parties. Interestingly, many participants in Glasgow said that they would be more likely vote if their vote may help prevent extremist parties (especially extremist right-wing parties) from gaining power. In Dundee, there was a consensus that voting might be increased if politicians spent more time finding out what the public wants – by approaching people in street/door to door and through online discussions – then attempted to deliver on this. A couple of people in this group also commented that they would be more likely to vote if more information was available about the choices at stake in elections and what parties are offering.

The issue of the 'honest' and 'genuine' politician was very important to participants – or 'the biggest point' as one person in Dundee put it – mainly because of what they saw as a lack of such leaders among the current political class. Participants would be much more likely to vote if they considered those representing them to be worthy of the title: 'Start being a bit more honest about what they're going to deliver and if they cannae do it, tell us.' (Dundee group)

Further, they wanted politicians who 'stand out from the crowd' and who were committed to their beliefs. They spoke of a number of Scottish politicians, including Donald Dewar and George Galloway as examples, but also singled out Boris Johnson, Dennis Skinner and Tony Benn as conviction politicians who they found appealing. Although these politicians come from different parts of the political spectrum, they were perceived as people who stood up to the establishment and pursued what they believed in.

At the end of each focus group, participants were asked to complete (in writing) the sentence, 'I would be more likely to vote if...' and their responses were collated and coded. Reflecting the themes already reported, the most common answer (given by around a third of group participants) was:

'If parties were more representative of the public/voters and more in tune with the issues they face.' In the Glasgow general public group in particular, there was a specific focus on politicians being more working class and/or more in touch with 'working people':

> [I would be more likely to vote if I trusted the politicians standing for election. However, I feel they are all out of touch with what is going on for the working people and I cannot relate to them and them with me.
>
> general public group, Glasgow

> The government were in line with the reality of the issues that people are facing – on a daily basis.
>
> general public group, Glasgow

The next most common responses were, respectively:

> 'If politicians were more honest/trustworthy/didn't lie just to get my vote' (mentioned by eight participants).

> 'If politicians followed through on pre-election promises/were held accountable for not doing so' (eight).

> 'If more information was available on different parties/what they stand for' (five).

> 'If I felt my vote counted/made a difference' (two).

[I would be more likely to vote if...] politicians were more honest and more straight-talking... there seems to be so much propaganda involved leading up to elections and they don't deliver what they promise.

Dundee group

[I would be more likely to vote if...] there was more accountability to do what you are voted in on. And MPs could be removed if they fail to do this.

young group, Glasgow

[I would be more likely to vote if...] manifestos were adhered to and MPs are not allowed to change them.

general public group, Glasgow

Other answers, each given by just one person, were if people were paid to vote; if voting was made easier, eg through the use of technology; and if there was a wider choice of parties. A participant in the Dundee group felt that there was a need for an independent body to vet manifesto commitments to ensure that politicians did not promise things that they could not deliver.

Voting in the independence referendum

Despite not discriminating between different types of election, the majority of participants in all three groups said that they would vote in the Scottish independence referendum in 2014. This reflected a notable difference in views about the referendum in comparison with other elections. The former was regarded as a one-off event of considerable importance, where there was much more at stake than parliamentary elections. Participants also felt that their vote may have some impact on the referendum result, whereas many were of the view that voting in elections would not make a difference to issues that mattered to them: 'This is very important for Scotland and its people... it's a big deal... there's no back-up plan with this one.' (Dundee group)

The intention to vote in the referendum is echoed in the results of several polls leading up to the referendum that show potential turnouts in the high 70 percentage points. The minority who said that they definitely would not vote in the referendum (all in the Glasgow groups) explained this in terms of not being Scottish and not feeling that they have a right to vote (two people); or not knowing enough about the issues at stake in the referendum to make an informed decision (one person).

CHAPTER THREE

A Deeper Look

OTHER FAIRLY CONSISTENT points emerged from these guided discussions with people who no longer saw any point in voting, in that they were not going to vote for any politicians because:

- Voting changes nothing normally, but it might in the independence referendum.
- Politicians are not like us and they don't really care about us.
- Political parties are all the same.
- Politics is dishonest.

There has always been distrust for politicians. Many of these things have been said universally for centuries and are important because democratic leaders are as prone to hubris as any other successful human being. One strength of democracy is that it shouts 'remember though art mortal' in the face of politicians on a daily basis. However, not so long ago, politicians were admired and revered as figures of status and respected by most. At the very least, they were seen as pillars of their local community, and at most as great men and woman who might make history. Surveys like Hansard's Democratic Audit indicate that the sentiments expressed by the non-voters in the focus groups are more widely held and heartfelt than at any time since the winning of universal suffrage.

The next section reviews these assertions to discover if these are just the cynicism of the crowd, the moaning myths of malcontents, or contain more. Considerations include whether people have real reason for holding these opinions and whether there is evidence to support or, alternatively, to challenge them. Hard truth or misconception, it is vital to understand why so many people are not voting, because it is eroding confidence in the practice which at the beginning of the 21st century seemed solid and reliable: that is the British state, the gradually evolving unwritten constitution, our leaders and the experts that seem(ed) to make society work. Whether individuals want to hasten its decline, repair it or move on the next thing, there is a need to delve more deeply into what is going on.

It may be that the system by which we run our society – representative democracy – is in serious crisis. In *The Confidence Trap*, David Runciman agrees with de Tocqueville that democracy is in a semi-permanent state of crisis, but often it is hard to know when such crises should be taken seriously. We must be sure of what is a real crisis that may lead to disaster, and what is merely something that will be solved by the flexibility and ingenuity of the system (Runciman 2014). This system has dealt with many real crises: from two World Wars and the Cold War to the near global banking collapse, but is still a system that works on faith. The vast majority of people have to believe in it, and if they stop believing, all sorts of morbid things begin to happen.

The independence referendum has provided a useful lens through which to view this problem because non-voters have suddenly become important. It is clear that they are likely to vote and may even decide the overall result. The 'missing million' have been identified as a group of target voters, which is something that never happens in most other elections. This, combined with a growing worry about the animosity towards politics and representative democracy as it is currently practised, makes such a study so timely. The referendum will come and go and might change many things, but being independent or being part of the union, is still unlikely to halt this decline in trust. It is important therefore to analyse what is happening and to develop some ideas on how to deal with the challenges in case the system is unable to heal itself.

Voting changes nothing

Russell Brand, celebrity TV presenter and stand-up comedian, was a surprise guest editor of the *New Statesman* magazine in October 2013. His editorial essay on 'a revolution in our thinking' and subsequent TV and radio appearances, particularly his *Newsnight* interview with Jeremy Paxman, caused a storm in the mainstream media, but a tidal wave on social media. In summary, Brand told people that they should stop voting as it changed nothing and legitimised a bad system. He was supported and lambasted in almost equal measure, labelled an irresponsible clown by some for abusing his celebrity status by encouraging young people to throw away what little power they had, praised by others as a visionary for shining a spotlight on what was so deeply wrong with politics and calling for big and fundamental change.

He articulated, in his unique and impressive manner, many of the views that the focus group members in Glasgow and Dundee held. They wanted things to change, and for some of them this was almost a desperate desire, but did not believe that voting would change anything. There have been relatively frequent changes of government at Westminster and Holyrood over the lifetime of all the focus group participants, even the youngest, so it is likely that from their own experience they perceive that voting can at times change governments.

What they must mean, as Brand implied, is that it does not matter who the government are, as whatever their political complexion, nothing changes for them. This 'nothing changes' trope feeds into the perception of political leaders that 'they are all the same' and 'not like us,' and that the issues talked about and argued over during an election are not those that affect the non-voting group. So what are the propositions from the non-voters and how real are they? This statement from the focus groups perhaps captured the perceived problem: If parties were more representative of the public/voters and more in tune with the issues they face.

In the Glasgow general public group in particular, there was a specific focus on politicians being more working class and/or more in touch with 'working people'. In order to explore this, four main aspects have been examined:

1   How representative politics is, including the backgrounds of the political representatives; how much they are like each other ('they are all the same') and how much they are like people that don't vote ('they are not like us').

2   The policy positions of the main parties at the last Scottish election through manifesto commitments: as the Scottish Parliament does not have power over some of the most significant issues of concern for non-voters – issues such as welfare, and those that impact jobs and wages, such industrial strategy and tax – UK policy platforms in 2014 were also analysed to better understand the difference between policy offers. (So how much are they 'all the same' on policy?)

3   How much politicians talk and listen to these groups. ('They are not interested in us and they do not listen to us.')

4   Has policy impacted on their lives and improved them or harmed them in any way? Policy claims are one thing, but what have been

the outcomes for these groups, and have things got better or worse? ('Nothing changes/ gets any better.')

They are not like us but the same as each other

'If the Civil Rights movement had been run by white people, black people would not have won those rights.' Rev Paul Chapman (friend and colleague of Dr Martin Luther King)

In summer 2013, Falkirk Labour Party, for the second time in as many years, became a serious source of concern for the Labour leadership. Having expelled Eric Joyce MP for drinking, fighting and being arrested, the party started the selection process for a new potential MP. Labour then became involved in a more sober, less violent but almost as ferocious conflict. Unite – the trade union and largest donor to the Labour Party – was accused of signing up union members to Falkirk Labour Party without their knowledge to marshall as many votes as possible in favour of the union's preferred candidate (BBC 2014). This played right into a story that the Tory party wanted to tell about dodgy union fixing and about Ed Miliband being unable to confront them because they were his paymasters. Miliband looked shaky for a day or two before hitting back, announcing a special conference to be held in March of the following year. At this he planned, and then pushed through, what he claimed were the biggest reforms of the Labour Party since Clause 4, by recasting the party's relationship with the trade unions, so that only affiliation fees that individuals specifically agreed could go to Labour.

The background to the Falkirk scandal had seen a growing feeling within some parts of the Labour Party that working-class people were no longer able to become elected representatives (Wheeler 2012). Several voices in the Labour Party, including the journalist Owen Jones, were pointing out that there was a clear return to the days when Parliamentarians had no lived life experience of the people they claimed to represent (Jones 2013). Calls for more working people were, at times, resisted predominantly by those with ambitions for office, but were not from that background. Progress – an internal New Labour faction established by Peter Mandelson – became the focus for much of this resistance against the push for more working-class MPs (Progress 2012).

Owen Jones and the unions established a think tank called Centre for

Labour and Social Studies (Class) to produce a policy agenda for this group, and Unite developed a strategy of active intervention to ensure that more people from working-class backgrounds were selected to become potential MPs (Workers Liberty 2012). Whether Falkirk was subject to an intended or an over enthusiastic targeting and implementation of that strategy is hard to say. However, the moves were controversial, the tactics criticised and scandal ensued. The motivation behind Unite's actions in Falkirk and in its other target seats was to bring a broader range of people into parliament against prevailing conditions, and the truth is that Labour Party selections have often been 'stitch ups' –whether by the party machine, prominent powerful individuals or particular groups. Politics is about power, and powerful people seek to entrench their power by placing their allies in other powerful positions. Perhaps Miliband had decided to change that, and if he genuinely has, he must be applauded. However, elements of Labour were not the only people worrying about whole swathes of the population not being represented in parliament or government. Ex-Conservative Prime Minister John Major made a speech in November 2013 saying that he was 'shocked at the privately educated elites' hold on power' (Wintour 2013).

The professionalisation of politics

What representation is has often been an interesting discussion point in political science. Does representation mean 'representative of' or on 'behalf of'? It might make sense to have both. It may be a good thing to have some highly educated and rhetorically skilled representatives advocating for others, but there is nothing as convincing as authenticity and people as the experts of their own experiences. It seems essential for people making laws and taking decisions on behalf of people to know what it is like to live the lives of those people – at least to some extent. Many of those who have turned their back on voting seem to sense this knowledge and resonance is missing, and that it affects them.

This is not only a deficit problem. It is not just a lack of people that have the 'lived life' experience of those they want to represent. It is true that the political elite have never been that much like the people, but participation in elections was greatest when they were more so. The problem is also one of a substantial narrowing of those that belong to the political elite, and the rise of the career politician, as those in political power are now much more likely to come from politically facilitating occupations. Certain occupations provide aspiring politicians with the contacts, knowledge, money, power, time and skills to become MPs or MSPs (Cairney 2007), such as working in think tanks, political parties, public affairs or campaigning in NGOs or the private sector or within trade unions. There is strong evidence that increasing professionalisation changes the nature of representation and perhaps misses out on much of the knowledge and experience of our population. It also has implications for how politics is communicated and entrenches 'the tricks of the trade', as explored in a later chapter.

Table 5 – MPs' Occupations 1979 to 2010

MPs from main parties (Conservative/Labour/Liberal Democrat)

	1979	1983	1987	1992	1997	2001	2005	2010
Number								
Professions	278	278	262	258	272	270	242	218
Barrister	67	69	57	53	36	33	34	38
Solicitor	29	35	31	30	28	35	38	48
Doctor	8	5	5	6	9	8	6	9
Civil service/local govt	30	27	22	26	37	35	28	18
Teachers: University/college	28	32	36	45	61	53	44	25
Teacher: school	49	43	48	57	65	64	47	24
Business	138	162	161	152	113	107	118	156
Miscellaneous	106	115	133	154	188	200	217	222
White Collar	9	21	27	46	72	76	78	84
Politician/Political organiser	21	20	34	46	60	66	87	90
Publisher/Journalist	46	45	42	44	47	50	43	38
Farmer	23	21	19	12	7	6	8	10
Manual Workers	98	74	73	63	56	53	38	25
Miner	21	20	17	13	13	12	11	7
Total	619	629	629	627	629	630	615	621
Percentage	%	%	%	%	%	%	%	%
Professions	44.9	44.2	41.7	41.1	43.2	42.9	39.3	35.1
Barrister	10.8	11.0	9.1	8.5	5.7	5.2	5.5	6.1
Solicitor	4.7	5.6	4.9	4.8	4.5	5.6	6.2	7.7
Doctor	1.3	0.8	0.8	1.0	1.4	1.3	1.0	1.4

	1979	1983	1987	1992	1997	2001	2005	2010
Percentage	%	%	%	%	%	%	%	%
Civil service/local govt	4.8	4.3	3.5	4.1	5.9	5.6	4.6	2.9
Teachers: University/college	4.5	5.1	5.7	7.2	9.7	8.4	7.2	4.0
Teacher: school	7.9	6.8	7.6	9.1	10.3	10.2	7.6	3.9
Business	22.3	25.8	25.6	24.2	18.0	17.0	19.2	25.1
Miscellaneous	17.1	18.3	21.1	24.6	29.9	31.7	35.3	35.7
White Collar	1.5	3.3	4.3	7.3	11.4	12.1	12.7	13.5
Politician/Political organiser	3.4	3.2	5.4	7.3	9.5	10.5	14.1	14.5
Publisher/Journalist	7.4	7.2	6.7	7.0	7.5	7.9	7.0	6.1
Farmer	3.7	3.3	3.0	1.9	1.1	1.0	1.3	1.6
Manual Workers	15.8	11.8	11.6	10.0	8.9	8.4	6.2	4.0
Miner	3.4	3.2	2.7	2.1	2.1	1.9	1.8	1.1

Source: Butler, Kavanagh, Cowley et al, *The British General Election of 2010 and previous editions*

The number of MPs that were manual workers before going into politics has dropped dramatically since 1979, from around 16 per cent then to four per cent in 2010. The number of MPs coming from the professions has also fallen from 45 per cent in 1979 to 35 per cent in 2010, and as the professions have declined, they have been replaced by MPs from other non-manual occupations. The rise of the career politician is noticeable in the growth of the number of MPs who come to Westminster already with a political background. In 1979, three per cent of MPs from the main parties were previously politicians or political organisers, compared to 14 per cent in 2010. This is much higher than any other specific field of occupation. MPs from a business background are usually Conservative, the fall in their numbers has been reversed since 2005 and they now form a quarter of the main parties' MPs.

Education

In 2010, over one third of our MPs had attended private school as children. The proportion varies by party, from 14 per cent of Labour MPs to 39 per cent of Liberal Democrat MPs, to 54 per cent of Conservative MPs. By comparison, nine per cent of pupils aged 11 and over in UK schools are in non-maintained (fee-paying) schools. Around three quarters of MPs elected in 2010 were university graduates.

Table 6 – Education of MPs elected in General Elections 1979 to 2010 (three main UK parties)

Per cent attending educational institution

		1979	1983	1987	1992	1997	2001	2005	2010
CON	Fee-paying school	73	70	68	62	66	64	60	54
	University	68	71	70	73	81	83	81	80
	Oxford & Cambridge	49	48	44	45	51	48	43	34
LAB	Fee-paying school	18	14	14	15	16	17	18	14
	University	59	53	56	61	66	67	64	72
	Oxford & Cambridge	21	15	15	16	15	16	16	17
LD	Fee-paying school	55	52	45	50	41	35	39	39
	University	45	65	73	75	70	69	79	81
	Oxford & Cambridge	27	30	27	30	33	27	31	28

Source: Butler, Kavanagh, Cowey et al *The British General Election of 2010 & previous editions*

The main change in the education of MPs over this period has been that less went to Oxbridge than in the past, although it is still over a quarter. In 1979, 225 MPs elected from the three main UK parties had been to Oxford or Cambridge, 36 per cent of these parties' MPs. At the 2010 election, 165 MPs elected from the three main UK parties (27 per cent) had an Oxbridge background.

At a UK Westminster level, four per cent of elected representatives come from manual worker backgrounds and a third went to private schools, compared with nine per cent in the population. Three quarters were university graduates and a quarter went to Oxbridge. It is hard to profile the missing million, but the general Scottish population is clearly very far removed from this picture of elected representatives, as can be seen in Tables 8 and 9. Perhaps, though, the Scottish Parliament has addressed this problem? That was certainly the claim and the expectation when its arrival was heralded at the turn of the 21st century. It was to be a place of new politics that not only brought power closer to ordinary Scots in locality, but also shared that power more widely within Scotland. Scots claim to be egalitarian, and seem to be proud of their working-class heritage, so it would makes sense if that was valued by the party selection processes and in the elections. There is no doubt that devolution presented a great opportunity to push back against the trends of exclusion and of a narrowing gene pool.

Table 7 – Formative occupation of MSPs, 1999–2011

	1999	2003	2007	2011
Professions	51.2	49.6	45.0	33.1
Business	17.3	14.0	15.5	17.7
Politics-Facilitating	18.1	24.8	23.3	28.2
Blue and White Collar Jobs	3.9	3.9	7.0	9.7
Miscellaneous	5.5	7.8	8.5	11.3

Source: (Cairney, Keating and Wilson, unpublished)

The Scottish Parliament has seen a steady decline in the power of the traditional professions of law, teaching and others as a launch pad for a political career, with a significant shift towards more 'politics-facilitating' backgrounds. There has been a slight increase in MSPs from blue and junior white-collar backgrounds, where the largest number of the Scottish population works. Census data from 2011 showed that over 40 per cent of the population were in socio-economic groups that might be described as those types of work.[1] Looking at the actual occupations reported in the census adds to the picture, with over 60 per cent of Scots working in jobs that might fall into that category. Just under ten per cent of MSPs originated in jobs like that. There is not a direct comparison in the data collected by Keating et al with classifications used in the census, and there are possible overlaps between the classifications, but by comparing the social class and occupation information. It is possible to arrive at a more composite picture.

[1] Group 4 is included here despite small employers including business people as many workers i.e. construction workers are self-employed own account workers.

Table 8 – Scottish population by socio-economic classification

National Statistics Socio-economic Classification (NS-SeC)	All people aged 16 to 74	1. Higher managerial, administrative and professional occupations: 1.1 Large employers and higher managerial occupations	1. Higher managerial, administrative and professional occupations: 1.2 Higher professional occupations	2. Lower managerial and professional occupations	3. Intermediate occupations	4. Small employers and own account workers
Scotland	3,970,530	65,396	278,832	802,545	513,038	294,610
per cent		1.6	7.0	20.2	12.9	7.4
grouped per cent			8.6	20.2	12.9	

National Statistics Socio-economic Classification (NS-SeC)	5. Lower supervisory and technical occupations	6. Semi-routine occupations	7. Routine occupations	8. Never worked and long-term unemployed: L14.1 Never worked	8. Never worked and long-term unemployed: L14.2 Long-term unemployed	L15 Full-time students
Scotland	326,930	616,404	514,036	124,530	74,100	360,109
per cent	8.2	15.5	12.9	3.1	1.9	9.1
grouped per cent			44.0		5	9.1

Source: Scotland's Census 2011

Table 9 – Scottish population by occupation type

Occupation	All people aged 16 to 74 in employment	1. Managers, directors and senior officials	2. Professional occupations	3. Associate professional and technical occupations	4. Administrative and secretarial occupations
Scotland	100.00 per cent	8.38 per cent	16.75 per cent	12.65 per cent	11.37 per cent
Occupation	5. Skilled trades occupations	6. Caring, leisure and other service occupations	7. Sales and customer service occupations	8. Process, plant and machine operatives	9. Elementary occupations
Scotland	12.52 per cent	9.71 per cent	9.31 per cent	7.69 per cent	11.61 per cent

Source: Scotland's Census 2011

Just over a quarter of Scots have gone to university or other higher education institutions, while around about the same amount have no qualifications at all (Census 2011). University graduates are represented almost threefold in parliament in relation to the actual population. There are a significant number of MSPs with no qualifications, particularly true of SNP members, and this is reflective of people in Scotland. Private school background is over represented, although not as high as at Westminster – in 2011 in Scotland, 4.5 per cent of the school population was educated in private schools and just over 15 per cent of MSPs were educated that way.

Table 10 – Educational backgrounds of MSPS 2011

Per cent	MSPS	Labour MSPS	SNP MSPS
State School	84.9	86.7	88.0
Private School	15.1	13.3	12.0
Oxbridge	1.6	0.0	2.9
Other HE	68.5	72.7	63.7
Other FE	13.7	21.2	11.6
None	16.9	6.1	21.7

Source: (Cairney, Keating and Wilson unpublished)

Scotland's political elite

It would be difficult to argue that there is no elite political class in Scotland. There is an elite drawn from the middle and political class, which some may find acceptable and maybe even desirable. It may be the case that our political leaders will use their education and privilege to good effect in pursuing the common good, but there is little evidence of that over the last few decades. The decline of working people representing themselves has coincided with a decline in their relative economic position and with their quality of life, as shown elsewhere in this book. It is true that the technological and economic forces that changed society gave an opportunity for those who at one time had to concede power to organised labour and their political representatives to now reclaim it for old interests, or to claim it anew for different sets of interests.

We have seen the rise and rise of the managerial class and their political representative (the professional politician) to the cost of the working class. Social and economic changes were both cause and effect of this power shift, which led to changes that have been managed more favourably for some groups than others, with those that have fared worst being those with the least access to power. This flags up an important flaw in our democracy – that it is not the government of the people, by the people for the people. Instead, it is government by a few people for some of the people, and the rest are beginning to opt out of a system upon which they can have no effect. It may be just a minority that it does not work for, but their disengagement damages the whole system.

Are their policies all the same?

Taking a steer from the focus groups, the things that seemed to be most important to these non-voters were security in work and in income as well as a good benefits safety net and affordable, secure housing. What is clear is that people feel as if they are living on the edge, without choices to change the precariousness of their lives. It is useful to compare parties to see how much their policy platform is the same, as claimed by non-voters. It is also important to see if realistic policies exist that might address the concerns of this group. Agencies and institutions that regard these things as important have very nearly come to a consensus on policy areas where some things could be done, such as approaches that would reduce insecurity and make people feel more equal, that reduce the influence of a 'them and us' society and a 'them and us' politics. These include:

- Skilful design of the tax and benefits system – recommended by the Institute of Fiscal Studies in their comprehensive review of the British Tax system (Mirrilees et al 2011).

- Industrial strategy to ensure higher paid, higher skilled work force, secure jobs and employment protection with collective bargaining – recommended by Scottish Trade Union Congress and the Reid Foundation (Boyd 2013) (Common Weal 2013).

- Extensive house building programme – recommended by Barker Review of Housing Supply commissioned by the last Labour Government (Barker 2004).

Table 11 – Summary of party manifesto commitments in
Scottish Parliament Election 2011

Policy Area	SNP	Labour	Conservatives	Liberal Democrats	Greens
Economy/ tax	Freeze council tax for next Parliament;	Freeze council tax for next two years;	Freeze council tax for next two years;	Freeze council tax for next two years;	Replace Council tax with land value tax;
	25,000 modern apprenticeships and 100,000 training places per year;	Abolish youth unemployment and create 250,00 jobs by end of decade;	£200 council tax cut for every pensioner household;	Generate £1.5bn from selling Scottish Water and making it a public benefit company;	Increase Scottish variable rate by 0.5p from 2013; Consider 'Hotel tax';
	£250m Scottish Futures fund focusing on young people and early years;	Scottish Futures job fund to create 10,000 work placements;	£140m Scottish business start-up fund; Maintain small business rate relief;	Replace Scottish Enterprise with Regional Development Bank;	At least 10 per cent of public spending to go through Social enterprise;
	Amend Scotland Bill to gain additional powers over issues like Corporation tax	Guaranteed modern apprenticeship for suitably qualified 16 to 18 year olds who want one. Living wage as an objective.	New Scottish minister for Enterprise and jobs	Superfast broadband in all parts of Scotland	Keep small business bonus, while giving councils share of business rate growth

Policy Area	SNP	Labour	Conservatives	Liberal Democrats	Greens
Health	Protect NHS Budget; Re-introduce minimum pricing of alcohol bill	Protect NHS Budget; Right to see cancer specialist within two weeks	Protect NHS Budget; Re-introduce prescription charges at £5	Protect free personal care; New two-week target for urgent referral for cancer diagnosis	NHS free at point of use with no privatisation; Support minimum pricing and strategic plan to reduce smoking
Justice	Maintain police numbers; Consult on options to reform police services; Roll out 'no knives, better lives' scheme	Six-month mandatory minimum jail sentence for carrying knife; Protect police office numbers; Create single national police force and single fire service	Maintain police numbers; End automatic early release from prison; Move to single police force and elect local police commissioners to listen to resident views.	Oppose single police force and fire and rescue service; Maintain police officer numbers; Reform prisons, with greater emphasis on preventing re-offending and involve voluntary sector	Focus on crime prevention; Oppose single police force; Presumption against very short sentences
Education	No university tuition fees; Continue reduction of class sizes especially P1 to P3; Expand pre-school support and create a new Sure Start Fund to improve life-chances for young Scots	No university tuition fees; Specialised training for up to 1,000 teachers, to boost literacy and numeracy standards; Give every young person right to quality training, stay in school or to go into further education until they are 18, by 2015	Introduce variable university graduate fee, capped at £4,000 annually with expectation of average charge of £3,600; Reduce school leaving age to 14, provided pupils sign up to a monitored apprenticeship or a full-time vocational or	No university tuition fees; £250m early years intervention fund; Provide opportunity for youngsters to attend college to do a course of their choice from the age of 14	No university tuition fees; Allow young people to study flexibly alongside work if they wish, with support to put their own small business ideas into practice; Give councils the 'resources they need' to keep local nurseries and schools open and class sizes down

Policy Area	SNP	Labour	Conservatives	Liberal Democrats	Greens
Education			technical training course; Allow educational charities, philanthropists, not-for-profit trusts and parents to set up new schools		
Constitution	Referendum bill on independ-ence; Amend Scotland Bill to extend powers of Scottish Parliament	Support increasing the borrowing powers set out in the Scotland Bill, in line with the recommen-dations of MSPs; Support devolving capital borrowing powers earlier than set out in the Scotland Bill	Support the provisions set out in the Scotland Bill on more tax, borrowing and other powers for Holyrood	Support the provisions set out in the Scotland Bill on more tax, borrowing and other powers for Holyrood	Renewed convention on Scottish devolution, with the public and civic organisa-tions in the driving seat instead of politicians; Multi-option referendum with choices including the status quo, a stronger Scottish Parliament with powers defined through a participative process, and full independence
Environment	Increase domestic electricity generation from renewables to 100 per cent by 2020, ensuring 130,000 jobs delivered in low-carbon economy;	80 per cent of energy to come from renewa-bles by 2020; Plans for new nuclear power stations 'considered on merit,' in terms of safety,	End Scottish government policy against new nuclear power – consider proposals for new stations but not on new sites;	Scotland to generate the equivalent of 100 per cent of Scotland's electricity consumption from renewable sources by 2025;	Renewable energy to meet Scotland's domestic energy demand by 2020; Close existing nuclear power stations at or before the end of their normal working lives,

Policy Area	SNP	Labour	Conservatives	Liberal Democrats	Greens
Environment	Oppose new nuclear power stations	environmental impact and community views	All public bodies to publish energy consumption details and commit to targets for cutting it	Oppose new nuclear power plants, while backing carbon capture and storage technology	with waste to be stored on site in secure, monitored and retrievable conditions
Transport	Edinburgh-Glasgow rail improvement programme and electrification of much of the central Scotland rail network; Take forward projects including Borders Railway and M8 Baillieston to Newhouse, M74 Raith Junction and M8, M73 and M74 network improvements	Reinstate Glasgow Airport Rail Link; Committed to deliver Aberdeen bypass, M8 Baillieston to Newhouse upgrade, and M74 Raith interchange	Make ScotRail franchise available for extended period of ten years, from next renewal, in return for savings, improved investment in rolling stock or better services; Abolish regional transport partnerships, with the exception of Strathclyde Partnership for Transport	Develop a fully-costed and timetabled plan to dual the A9 to Inverness; Fairer fares charter for rail passengers	Save almost £2bn by scrapping the Aberdeen West Peripheral Route and new Forth road bridge, while repairing the existing one; £75m-a-year to cut fares
Housing (not in original SPICE briefing but gleaned from party manifestos)	New approach to financing new house building. Scottish Housing Bond and accessing pension funds to secure additional Investment.	Meet Scottish Housing Quality Standard. Mortgage indemnity scheme reduce the level of deposit required of first-time	Reinstate a 'modernised Right to Buy.' Stock transfer by councils to housing Associations with tenant approval. Weighting or local people	Bring empty homes back into use with grant of up to £10K. New Funding for social housing from bonds and Pension Funds. Shared Equity & Indemnity for first time	£100m a year national programme of home energy efficiency. Further restrict the Right to Buy, Take over management of properties from irresponsible landlords.

Policy Area	SNP	Labour	Conservatives	Liberal Democrats	Greens
Housing (not in original SPICE briefing but gleaned from party manifestos)	Levy on empty houses bring in £30 million extra to fund further council house building guarantee to retain secured tenancies at affordable Tenant Deposit Scheme,	buyers to only ten per cent. Infrastructure fund to encourage private developers to build. New taskforce to identify housing needs. Improve the private rented sector.	and people with a proven family connection in Social Landlords' allocation of housing.	buyers. Liberalise landlord allocation policy.	Support local authorities who use prudential borrowing for housing. New build delivered by a range of social landlords al marriage

Source: Spice Briefing Scottish Election 2011

Table 11 summarises manifesto commitments of the five main parties in the Scottish Parliament 2011 election, as set out in a briefing by the Scottish Parliament Information Centre (SPICE). This briefing, published a few days after the election, took account of the arguments and topics that were fought over in that campaign. It seems important that housing was not even considered in this briefing. Comparing the policy areas that might impact most on non-voters is summarised below.

Tax and benefit

These government functions are mainly reserved at Westminster, so it is unsurprising that there is little to show. Although council tax rates where a big issue during the election campaign, all the parties seem to shadow each other on the 'council tax freeze' – except for the Greens, who want to have a Land Value Tax (considered a very radical move) and to raise more tax with the Scottish Parliament's tax varying power on the income tax rate.

Housing

The original Spice briefing had no mention of housing policy, despite it being a major concern for non-voters, most likely because it was hardly mentioned in the election campaign. There are several similarities, however, across parties: indemnity on deposits for first time buyers, and methods of trying to bring in use or to generate revenue from 'empty properties,' a focus for the Greens. The Tories have a stand out difference on bringing back 'right to buy,' although this is not a policy that would appeal to the non-voters. The SNP have the strongest commitment to building houses through their council house programme; Labour, Tories and Lib Dems seem to want more private housing, and the SNP and Greens emphasise social housing. None have what could be called radical large-scale house building programmes.

Industrial/wages

SNP and Labour propose similar suggestions on creating work for young people through apprenticeships. The Conservatives wanted to establish a business fund and the Lib Dems wanted a National Investment Bank. Greens wanted government procurement to go through more social enterprises.

There are very few standout differences between the two big parties (SNP and Labour) in Scottish politics in the areas that have been high-lighted. The Green Party, if it had power, may well do something that might impact significantly on the lives of the non-voters. So why do people not vote for the Greens? Such a small party arguably is so limited by its lack of resources that it cannot effectively get its message to this group, and is more likely to focus on its core vote of middle-class liberals in the nicer parts of Edinburgh and Glasgow. The next question might be why do the larger parties not tap into this potential extra million votes, something that will be addressed later.

Westminster

It might be reasonable to question this comparison on the grounds that UK and Westminster politics still affect the political culture and attitudes of Scotland, at least as much as the young Parliament in Edinburgh does.

The truth is that significantly more Scots go out and vote in the UK General Election than at a Scottish election, and the policy themes that potentially have the biggest impact are also still driven from Westminster, namely tax and welfare, and parts of economic strategy. In order to test the claim that little would change, we really have to consider both institutions and the policies and people that are associated with them.

Qualification and limitations

We will now individually review what have been identified as significant policy areas and see where party and government policy sits on each of these in 2014 in Westminster and, where relevant, to Holyrood. This is not straightforward or empirical, but by searching through various statements, speeches and publications, it is possible to arrive at approximations of where parties stand on these large policy themes. These sources were used to try to build up a summary picture of the policy positions of each of party and to assess variance against each other, but also against potentially different policies that may be more beneficial to the groups who do not vote. The coalition is included as a reference point, to try to account for the effect that government has on policy. There is inevitably a reactive and interactive effect of party policy formation and communication, as one party will make an announcement and the others react to it.

This exercise aims to assess the 'closeness' of policy of the main political actors, to try and arrive at some idea of the choice of policy platform offered to voters. The focus has been made on parties that people may think they are voting for to form a government, but smaller parties can be important. In Scotland the Greens have a realistic chance of becoming influential in future coalition government, which is unlikely in Westminster. However, for this exercise, the Lib Dems are looked at as part of the Coalition government and the Greens are not assessed. It is relatively easy to assess the approach of the Coalition Government as they are pursuing a particular line of policy in government, introducing legislation and producing budget and government statements.

The Labour Party is in opposition at Westminster and Holyrood. They are starting to build up policy positions for their manifesto for the 2015 General Election by carrying out an extensive policy review. The Labour Party is behaving as oppositions usually do, in either not having settled on definite positions, or not fully revealing many areas of policy, instead often reacting to policy announced by the Coalition. It has been possible to arrive at an approximation of their positions through published policy documents (limited) and various statements and comments coming from Shadow cabinet members. Where policy is clearly reserved at Westminster – such as Tax and Welfare – UK Labour Party policy is taken where it overlaps, as on Industrial policy. There is a fusion of UK and Scottish policy and for fully devolved matters, Scottish Labour Party policy is explained.

The SNP have a majority Government in the Scottish Parliament. Their White Paper on an independent Scotland, 'Scotland's Future', gives a broad description of what they aspire to do with full independent state powers, and for devolved matters this can be checked against what they have done as a Government since 2007. Various working groups and investigations set up by the government give more detail on their positions.

a) Tax and benefit system

Tax and welfare policy is predominantly made and implemented at Westminster. The Scottish Parliament has effective control over council tax through the system of funding local government set business rates and reliefs, and can vary the base tax rate by up to three pence up or down. These powers will be added to when the 2012 Scotland Act comes into force in 2016.

UK Conservative–Liberal Democrat Coalition Government on tax and benefits

Analysis of the 2013 autumn budget statement assesses the recent position of the Coalition Government in its undertaking of an extensive overhaul of the benefit system, specifically the introduction of universal benefit that along with other changes, particularly the removal of the inflation linked rise, is estimated to increase child poverty in the UK by about 200,000 households – reverting to 2001 Levels by 2017/18 (Thompson 2013). This is expected to save £18 billion per year in 2014/15. The Government also introduced an overall cap on the amount of benefits to be paid, administered mostly through housing benefit, and introduced the high profile 'bedroom tax' (spare room subsidy), reducing housing benefit if social housing tenants have what is considered a 'spare room'.

Labour Party on tax and benefits

According to the One Nation Economy Policy Document's website, Labour say that if they are elected in 2015 they will cap structural social security spending as part of each Spending Review so that it is properly planned and controlled, and will also reverse the Bedroom Tax, with a funded plan to do so without additional borrowing (Labour Party 2013).

Liam Byrne MP, in a speech reported in the *Guardian*, made in August 2013 when he was Shadow Secretary for Work and Pensions, alleged that Labour wants to get universal credit and other major schemes back on track, rather than to scrap them altogether. Byrne also said that Labour would focus on cutting the overall benefits bill by getting people back into jobs through welfare-to-work schemes, and argued that 'anyone who can work should work'.

Scottish National Party on tax and benefits

The Scottish Government's White Paper on independence states (Scottish Government 2013):

> The tax and welfare systems are key levers in tackling inequality – both are strongly interlinked and should be considered as fundamentally part of the same system. Welfare and tax policy should therefore be developed in tandem to ensure policy integration and alignment.

It promises that a SNP Government in an independent Scotland will:

- Halt the further rollout of Universal Credit and Personal Independence Payment in Scotland, and remove housing benefit from the single payment.

- Restore it as a separate benefit and maintain direct payments to social landlords. Restore the ability of claimants to receive individual support rather than single household payments.

- Equalise the earnings disregard between first and second earners and continue such an approach into any longer term reforms.

- Ensure that benefits and tax credits increase in line with inflation to avoid the poorest families falling further into poverty.

Summary

On welfare there are differences between the Coalition Government and Labour, for example on 'bedroom tax,' but the difference seems to be more about efficiency of implementation rather than the overall approach. Each party are very similar in their approach to cutting spending, integrating benefit and in treating welfare as a dependency that disincentives work. The SNP are the only one of the three entities who talk about integrating the tax and benefit system, and that actively oppose the reforms of Universal Benefits.

b) Tax

UK Conservative–Liberal Democrat Coalition Government on tax

It is probably safe to say that the Coalition Government does not seek to substantially change the current tax system. Their approach is to change rates and allowances within the existing structures, so on income tax they raised the bottom allowance so that people have to earn more before paying tax on income, and they have removed the 50p tax rate on earnings over £150k. They have also reduced corporation tax (Conservative Party 2014) and cut employer National Insurance contributions (UK Government 2014). There is frequent rhetoric about corporate tax avoidance and attempts to persuade companies and 'tax havens' to be more transparent, but there is nothing in the way of legislation. The Coalition put up VAT to its highest ever rate when first in office, and it has stayed at this level (UK Government 2014). While the Lib Dems support a mansion tax, they cannot make it Government policy, due to Conservative opposition.

Labour Party on tax

Again, the Labour Party has no proposals to alter the structure of the current tax system (Labour Party 2013), but they do have some headline proposals to legislate against tax avoidance. Ed Balls (Shadow Chancellor) announced in January 2014 that they would restore the 50p top rate of tax for highest earners, previously removed by the Coalition (Oborne 2014). While earlier in the Parliament Labour spoke often of cutting the VAT rate, this has appeared less in party rhetoric since 2013. Labour also want to apply a windfall tax to bankers' bonuses and will reverse the corporation tax reductions, as well as introducing a Mansion Tax and reintroducing the lower 10p rate bottom band.

SNP on tax

SNP have a slightly two-faced approach to tax. On the one hand refusing to commit to restoring the 50p tax rate and having a lower corporation tax level than London and no position on a mansion tax, but on the other, in what appears to be a direct contrast to that Conservative position, they are committed to completely overhauling the current UK tax system should they achieve independence. The SNP may be in the historic situation of receiving a mandate to create a new state, and such a mandate means that more ambitious tax reform would be possible. That is certainly what the SNP commit to in their White Paper when they state they:

> ... plan to develop a new tax system for Scotland to better meet key policy objectives, based on the design principles of a modern and efficient system set out by the Fiscal Commission.

The White Paper goes on to say how that process of creating a new tax system will be guided, including:

> The tax system should be built around Scottish circumstances; the tax and welfare systems are key levers for tackling inequality; appropriate tax rates maximise receipts by creating the optimal level of economic activity and revenue-raising potential. The Scottish Government should assess the optimal balance of tax rates and bases for key taxes, such as business and employee taxes; an open and consultative approach with industry, independent experts, employer groups, the trade unions, and the general public should be adopted when designing the system.

Summary

The Labour Party and the Coalition Government disagree about where they put the emphasis on revenue raising and of the impact of their policies on the economy and society. There is a clear difference on the top rate of tax and on corporation tax rates. SNP align with the Coalition on the reduction of top rate and corporation tax, but only the SNP are committed to a fundamental re-creation of the tax system. While it could be said that they have no option if they are to build a new country, they could have adopted the UK system and placed different emphases on bands and rates within existing types of activity. SNP have also prioritised the need to integrate the tax and benefit system. It would appear that because of the circumstances created by the independence debate, SNP are not as constrained by the existing structures in the same way that the UK Labour Party or the Coalition Government. Of course for SNP and Labour, these are only statements of commitments at this particular time, but the ability to make statements indicates where they feel they have political space.

c) Industrial strategy

UK Conservative–Liberal Democrat Coalition on industry

In March 2012, Vince Cable – Lib Dem Business Secretary – decried the Coalition Government for their lack of industrial strategy in a leaked letter to 10 Downing Street. It seems the case that Cable has won that fight against his Tory partners and has been able to develop an interventionist industrial policy for key sectors of automotive, aerospace and life sciences: the Business Department says that £4bn of Government money was committed to the industrial strategy in 2013 (Rigby 2013). There are still some Tories who are resistant to the Government meddling in the economy, but their influence seems to be waning. Even on wages policy, a one-time 'third rail' issue for the Conservative Party, there seems to be support for an increased minimum wage, although no action yet (Watson 2014). The Coalition says it will enact legislation to ring-fence retail banking away from investment banking, but this will probably not be completed until 2019, and they are against limiting market shares for banks. There are ongoing moves to liberalise the Labour market with a new employment status of shares in return for giving up employment rights (BBC 2013). Besides that, rhetoric in support of green investment and low carbon business from opposition days has not been turned into actual policy in Government.

Labour Party on industry

Labour seems to have a strategy of supporting small and medium sized business as 'the job creators in the UK economy' as opposed to large companies, saying that:

> In an era when money is tight we must prioritise support for the hundreds of thousands of small businesses that are struggling, not the biggest businesses that have seen large tax cuts in recent years. These are the businesses whose innovation and dynamism we are relying on to drive our economy on but which politicians too often think don't matter to our future.
>
> Labour Party 2013

Labour set out to do this through a network of local business support banks and a National Investment Bank, and a freeze of business rates (Labour Party 2013). They promise to break up banks, separating retail banks from investment banks if the Coalition's proposal to ring-fence the separation has not worked by 2015 (Martin 2014). Labour also want to limit the market share that any retail bank can have through the Competition Commission (Labour Party 2013), are keen to support green technology development – seeing green industry as an opportunity for direct support to industry – and want to set up a Green Investment Bank. On pay, they support the rollout of a living wage by requiring listed companies to report on whether they pay it, along with having transparency of executives' pay and the publication of pay ratios for all listed companies. In general, they want increased regulation of labour markets, with outlawing zero hour contracts a key policy, and co-operation with trade unions. It must be said that most of this is UK-level policy and it seems hard to find separate new policy on industry from Scottish Labour.

SNP on industry

The SNP state that, 'The current Scottish Government will develop a new industrial strategy for Scotland.' They say a key priority will be to rebalance and reindustrialise Scotland's economy.

This strategy aims to secure a number of benefits, including: boosting high-value jobs through increased manufacturing activity; promoting innovation – although manufacturing firms account for only 12 per cent of Scottish (onshore) output, they account for 66 per cent of business R&D spending; addressing geographical disparities – the decline in manufacturing has contributed to geographical imbalances across Scotland. Increasing manufacturing activity in a local area will help develop clusters of economic activity and support local supply chains; boosting exports – around 62 per cent of Scottish international exports are manufactured and a greater focus on internationalisation across the economy will help boost competitiveness and support jobs.

This is with a strong commitment to 'green growth.' The SNP want a formal tripartite arrangement with government, trade unions and business, and therefore support a regulated labour market with strong trade unions and collective bargaining. They seek to establish a National Convention on Employment and Labour relations, bringing together labour market regulation and other employment-related policies in a forum, and to legislate for employee representation on company boards. Current Scottish Government plans to reverse recent changes introduced at Westminster that reduce key aspects of workers' rights, and their policy on banking reform appear to be to accept the rules that a UK government might put in place, or perhaps to jointly negotiate between the two governments; they are overall keen to maintain a single market for banking across the current UK area.

> We will work on a closely harmonised basis with the UK regulators, delivering an aligned conduct regulatory framework, to retain a broadly integrated market across the Sterling Area. The regulatory approach will include the application of single rulebooks and supervisory handbooks. (Scottish Government 2013)

Summary

With a close look, it is easy to identify fundamental differences between the different parties' approaches to industrial development, although the influence of the Lib Dems and particularly Vince Cable in the Coalition Government makes the picture less clear.

One thing that can be said is that, probably in part as a response to the financial crash, often seen as a result of deregulation, the days of *laissez-faire* British Governments have gone – if they ever really existed. All parties believe in intervention, although the Coalition seems to invest in particular industries seen as strategic, and Labour has a focus on SMEs, maybe as a reaction against the possible monopolising of large corporations. Labour also sees it as important to restructure the economy away from finance and to create space for SMEs to take up that relinquished economic capacity. SNP seem to want to restructure the economy in a similar way, although the omission of a preferred option on banking is important. The Coalition still maintains a 'light touch' on banking and sees gradual and 'soft' banking restructure as the way ahead.

The SNP are the only party to want a tripartite (trade union, business, government) development of industrial policy, which may seem surprising, as Labour has formal links with unions. Both see proper labour market regulation as important. The Tories unsurprisingly are actively deregulating the labour market, except for what might be a changing position on wages policy but only rhetorically up to the time of writing. SNP and Labour are close on wages, with the SNP perhaps having more space to make stronger commitments towards a living wage.

Different or the same?

One of the reasons that people in the focus groups said that they saw no point in voting was that they could see little difference in the political parties. In their eyes, there is no choice. 'They are all the same' is a cliché when it comes to criticism of politicians as a group. Clichés often become so for good reason – but what do they actually mean by 'all the same'? How do we understand this problem and therefore suggest remedies? The above examination of policy offers from the parties reveals some major themes that may have an effect on areas that our focus group members said they were most concerned about: namely work, pay and job security, housing and living from one pay check to the next. So how do party policies shape up on the 'not different' charge? It depends at what level and in what detail it is viewed from.

A reasonably detailed policy analysis clearly shows difference between the parties. Of course a large difference is the SNP's ability to claim that it can almost start from scratch, and in reality any transitions that they claim they can make will be at least as technically challenging as such a transition would be for the UK. Existing systems of tax, benefit and economic structure will still be in operation and have to be altered for this to be achieved. It is true that if the SNP won a Yes vote, this mandate – combined with the lesser concentration of institutional resistance in Scotland (i.e. smaller CBI, reduced influence of the city of London, tiny Tory party, smaller hostile media) – would mean that the political space for any sort of large-scale change should be considerably greater than at a UK level. They can talk about a wholly remade tax system, integrating with a benefit system and a tripartite approach to industrial strategy while they restructure the economic model. To voters this may seem more plausible, if they can achieve a mandate.

The SNP are close to Labour on most of their stated aims for the type of political economy they both claim to want, but the SNP can arguably be more ambitious because of the potential for increased political space that no UK party can foresee. There are also clear differences between what might be called the parties of the left, SNP and Labour and the more centre-right Coalition parties, in terms of vision as well as regarding tactics on the type of economic structures they desire, with Labour and the SNP aiming for more redistributive, higher wages and more job security that may potentially impact on the missing million. Where Labour and the Coalition seem closest is on the matter of Welfare and Benefits, both at a UK level where the power remains, and at a Scottish level where Scottish Leader Johann Lamont's rhetoric on universalism caused a storm in September 2012 when she said it was time to end 'the something for nothing' culture. Labour have not signalled any move back from that position on universalism (Taylor 2012).

So what do the missing million see when they look at political parties? Of course none are likely to undertake the detailed policy analysis that has happened here. What this does show is that even below the surface, the picture is complicated. Labour is close to the Coalition on Welfare. The Tories are close to the SNP on Tax. SNP are close to Labour on the type of political economy they desire for the nation. There are no clear divides. Even on purely a policy judgement, it is easy to see why someone could conclude that all parties are the same, because it needs a high level of analysis to be able to separate them out. Political parties know this might be a problem and often seek differentiation through totemic policies. There have been some totemic policy differences between political parties that might have helped to counter the view that 'they are all the same' and 'voting changes nothing.' Minimum wage is one, introduced by the New Labour Government of 1997 –always opposed by the Tories but not now. SNP Government introduced free prescription charges and free student tuition fees, now seemingly opposed by the Scottish Labour Party, and there are many who think these symbolic policies may have been important in the SNP electoral success, which saw them winning a minority Government in 2007 and a majority in 2011.

But these policies, however powerful or symbolic, do not seem to connect with those who do not vote. Parties do not present a distinct, coherent basket of policies connected to each other in any identifiable way. Many of the policies are interchangeable between parties, depending on what time they are being looked at; they jockey and manoeuvre for the same group of voters, at times overlapping and intersecting. There is no obvious story to tell except perhaps the one about independence. Politicians have little to say to the missing voters and even if they did, do not try to talk to them, as will be considered in the next chapter.

This analysis runs alongside the idea that important swing voters are happy to fit within this narrow band of political possibilities. Any party that moved beyond this centrist consensus would be punished at the polls, only to be replaced by a party slightly more fitting for the current political consensus. The political system may have imprisoned the parties in a very tight space and in doing so excluded so many that it is starting to erode our democracy.

The impact of policy

The ultimate test of whether people are being represented or not is how political power is being used to make their lives better. Long before the recession started the so-called booming economy was shifting much more of the proceeds of that boom to the people who most resembled MPs. The way the economy had been structured and regulated was in real terms taking from those that have given up on voting. Incomes of low-income households grew by just 0.3 per cent a year from 2003 to 2008, even while the UK economy grew at 1.4 per cent a year. This income stagnation was caused by flat-lining wages for both men and women, leaving tax credits as the only source of income growth among this group. From about 2003 onwards, wages at the bottom end of the labour market disconnected from productivity growth and fell in real terms (Resolution Foundation 2012). Between 2008 and 2013, real average income fell for Scots by 9.9 per cent (Neate 2013).

Table 12 – Trends in household income by Income Group,
mid-1980s to late 2000s

Average annual percentage change in real household income			
Country	Total Population	Top Decile	Bottom Decile
UK	2.1	2.9	0.5

Source: An Overview of Growing Income Inequalities in OECD Countries
http://www.oecd.org/els/soc/49499779.pdf

In the UK, while full-time earnings at the 90th percentile increased from £662 a week in 1984 to £1,007 a week in 2011, wages at the tenth percentile grew from just £218 to £279 over the same period (Resolution Foundation 2012). The problem with low pay is that the labour share of GDP has become much more concentrated at the middle to top of the labour market. The cost of housing also rocketed in social, as well as private, rented accommodation. The Local Authority median local reference rent (used to calculate a fair rent for Housing Benefit) was £64 per week in 2000. By 2011 it was £94, an increase of 68 per cent (Scottish Government 2013). Over the same period, general inflation was approximately 35 per cent. The changes to welfare have led to the Trussell Trust reporting a 170 per cent rise in the use of UK food banks from 2012 to 2013 (Trussell Trust 2013). Wages fell and the most basic cost of living – a home – rose for this group with what seems a concerted reduction of the safety net of a welfare system. Policy and politics was not working for many people despite the 'people's party' being in power for much of that time. Where else to turn to?

CHAPTER FOUR

Can You Hear Us?

Political marketing and segmenting the population

ONE REASON THAT the 'missing million' hear nothing relevant is that no one is trying to talk to them. Modern political campaigning has borrowed a large number of techniques from advertising and marketing in identifying target audiences and tailoring political messages at that target group – focusing effort and resources to connect with that group, and neglecting everyone else. These messages are delivered through leaflets drops and local media but are also the messages that the politicians repeat tirelessly in media appearances and speeches, via party political broadcasts and through national advertising campaigns, such as billboards.

Target groups are identified through detailed market surveys and polling done face to face, online and by telephone. For example, the Labour Party might want to find people who identified as Lib Dem in the past, but might be considering voting Labour. They then may use methods that marketers use to divide up the population, using behavioural data and allocating 'types' to those people, usually by postcode area. Using focus groups to discuss with these possible targets, they will hone understanding of their concerns and test messages that might work with that 'type.' The objective is to be able to identify as small as possible a target audience that your party can convince to vote for you, and if they did, that would enable an election victory. In marketing jargon, breaking down the population like this to deliver more specific and meaningful messages is known as segmentation; in politics it is also driven by attempting to concentrate resources to have the greatest return.

This group can be defined in a number of different cross-cutting ways. First and most, they must vote. This is significant because it is part of the 'don't vote, don't count, don't vote' egg and chicken situation described earlier. Second, they are not guaranteed or heavily committed to vote for your party or one of the other parties. Parties see it as a waste of resource to try and communicate with people that do not vote but also those whose votes are either 'in the bag' or never going to shift from another party. The people who may change from how they voted before are the famous swing voters, but being a swing voter alone is not enough. You must live in a constituency where the race is close enough for those voters' 'swing' to make a difference. These are the 'golden voters.'

Using data on everything from shopping habits, type of housing to news consumption, people were grouped together as potential 'swing groups' and surveyed and focus grouped again to see what their concerns are and what might convince them to vote one way or another. We can safely say that millions upon millions of pounds of political advertising and manpower are put into finding out what these people want, then convincing them that any particular party can deliver it.

Let's look at the Westminster system first. It has helped to dominate and shape the Scottish political culture for so long, and while the Scottish Election campaigns are slightly different and are evolving over time, many of the techniques derive from UK General Elections and are still relevant to Scottish Parliament Elections. The differences will be examined later.

The 'First Past the Post' system of Westminster elections means that the constituencies that make up the UK Parliament often have concentrated populations of one type of voter or another, which will be enough to ensure that that seat is very unlikely to change hands. This means that urban ex-industrial central belt areas (like Motherwell and Wishaw) almost always return Labour MPs (who dominate Scottish representation at Westminster). More rural Highland and Borders areas, or affluent city suburbs such as Edinburgh South West, return SNP, Lib Dem, or Tories in the past. Just as the North of England predominantly return Labour MPs and the South of England Tories. Because of the way the votes are counted under the First Past the Post system, the winner only requires a simple majority in their constituency, so if a particular party has a concentration of votes within that areas, and three or more candidates split the opposing vote, then it is almost impossible for any other party to hope to win there. These are the so-called 'safe seats'. Swing voters in safe seats are not a target for parties, as they will not affect the result.

There are other seats where the concentration of one party's votes is not high enough to guarantee a win. The seat could go two ways or more. These are referred to as marginal seats, swing seats, battleground seats or, as the parties will call them, target seats.

Table 13 – Top five highest spend per voter Scottish constituencies in 2010 UK General Election

Constituency	All Party Spend	Spending Per Vote	Type of Seat	Turnout
Edinburgh South	79305.8	£1.81	Lab/LD marginal	73.8
Dumfriesshire, Clydesdale and Tweeddale	78749.34	£1.72	Three way marginal Con/Lab/LD marginal	68.9
Glasgow North	71293.79	£1.71	Lab/LD marginal	67.3
Angus	70372.57	£1.70	SNP/Con marginal	66.9
Argyll and Bute	69880.26	£1.58	Four way marginal, principally LD/Con	66.4

Source: Electoral Reform Society, Penny for your Vote

Table 14 – Five lowest spends per vote Scottish constituencies 2010 UK General Election

Constituency	Overall Spend	Spending Per Vote	Seat Type	Turnout
Motherwell and Wishaw	9759.99	£0.25	Lab safe seat	58.5
Cumbernauld, Kilsyth and Kirkintilloch East	10299.95	£0.25	Lab safe seat	64.3
Rutherglen and Hamilton West	11822.07	£0.29	Lab safe seat	58.5
Coatbridge, Chryston and Bellshill	12780.27	£0.31	Lab safe seat	59.4
Kilmarnock and Loudoun	13759.06	£0.32	Lab safe seat	62.0

Source: Electoral Reform Society, Penny for your Vote (Electoral Commission Data)

The top and the bottom constituency are stand out examples of problems presented by the 'key seat strategies' of political parties. Only certain types of Scots living in certain places are ever targeted and courted for their votes. Motherwell, with high levels of unemployment and deprivation, is a very safe Labour seat, with Frank Roy returning as their MP in 2010 with 61.1 per cent of the vote; his nearest rival Marian Fellows, SNP, only getting 18.2 per cent. While in Edinburgh South West, perhaps the most affluent constituency in Scotland, including areas of Edinburgh such as Morningside and the Grange, was a Labour seat with a majority of only 405 votes. It was also an open seat, with the incumbent, Nigel Griffiths, standing down. It required only a 0.5 per cent swing for the Lib Dems to take the seat, and was top of Lib Dems' targets in Scotland, but was also a target for the Conservatives. On the day, Labour held the Lib Dems to a swing of only 0.1 per cent, and Ian Murray became a Labour MP with a majority of only 316 votes over Lib Dem candidate Fred Mackintosh – 34.7 per cent to 34 per cent. The Conservative candidate Neil Hudson, despite outspending all other candidates, trailed third with 21.6 per cent of the vote. With such an active, close-fought campaign in Edinburgh South, it is hardly surprising that the turnout there was over 15 per cent greater than in Motherwell and Wishaw

It is not only the huge discrepancy in spend that shows how swing voters in marginal seats are courted by parties. The whole political agenda – the issues that are fought over, the way the discussion are framed, the language that is used, the symbols and the metaphors – are all shaped by this highly targeted manner of doing politics. The policy platforms examined earlier in this book overlap because 'voter targets' of the parties overlap.

The Conservative Party in the 1980s was taking regular advice from the very successful advertising agency Saatchi and Saatchi, which helped Margaret Thatcher identify 'Essex Man' as a target group of swing voters. This set the trend to give extra special groups of voters' collective names and brands. Like many things in politics, it helped if they could be alliterative.

In his 1996 Labour Party conference speech, Tony Blair told of meeting a self-employed electrician polishing his Ford Sierra:

> His Dad voted Labour, he said. He used to vote Labour, too. But he'd bought his own house now. He'd set up his own business. He was doing very nicely. 'So I've become a Tory,' he said.

This meeting between Blair and the 'sparky' may have taken place, but most likely did not. This was an apocryphal description of target swing voters that New Labour pollsters had discovered would have to be won back to enable Labour to return to government. Thereafter there was a parade of composite people to whom political resources would be targeted:

Essex Man Tory target, particularly in Basildon, in 1992. Helped save John Major.

Sierra Man Subsequently the more alliterative Mondeo Man, this was the hard-working family guy who washed his Sierra on a Sunday morning. Labour target in 1997 landslide.

Worcester Woman Crucial swing voter in provinces with the key marginal of Worcester, the new target for the Tories in 2003.

Pebbledash People William Hague's unsuccessful alternative to Worcester Woman, married couples, aged 35–50 who owned homes in the suburbs.

Schoolgate Mums Labour's target in 2005 to focus on those who stayed at home or worked part time and picked up children from school.

Asda Mums Variation of schoolgate mums, but more focus on working woman, targeted by both parties in 2010.

And now there is **Aldi Mum**, described by Labour Shadow Cabinet Member Caroline Flint in a 2013 speech. Aldi Mum is a middle-aged, middle-class woman feeling the squeeze of recession, once upwardly mobile but now afraid of going backwards. Works in a public sector job, but not having had a pay rise for years, is cutting back on luxuries once purchased from the local delicatessen (luxuries Flint described as 'prosciutto and prosecco') and now does a 'double shop' at a regular supermarket like Sainsbury's and another at a discount one such as Aldi or Lidl.

None of these groups, up to now, could be used to describe the missing million. As the parties segment the UK population again and again, large groups of people, predominantly those with least access to power and influence, become increasingly distant from the political process. Of course there is an attitude that accepts this is the direction of travel of modern politics, but the unintended consequences may not just be unfair, they may actually undermine representative democracy.

Those running the Scottish referendum campaigns have begun to realise that a high turnout is likely and that people who do not normally vote will do so this time. This will mean that the missing million will have an effect on the outcome and party strategists are now applying these techniques to that group. It may be that you have made it as a voter when you are classified in this way by a politician, for example, by Jim Murphy:

> People I would call the 'copers'. Those people only ever one wage packet away from hardship. I'm thinking of the mum I met working at the all-night Asda, who kisses her kids goodnight and goes to work. That midnight mum and so many others are entitled to know how much they will have to pay for the SNP's dreams.
>
> JIM MURPHY MP Shadow Defence Secretary, March 2013

It is as yet unclear whether they are 'copers' or 'midnight mums,' but the previous penchant for mums and alliteration and the battle over the female vote in the referendum suggests the latter.

Scottish electoral systems and campaigning

The 2011, Scottish Parliament Elections was a painful experience for the Labour Party. They lost 20 constituency seats to the SNP with what they saw as their leading talents thrown out of the Parliament. They had to rely on list votes to bring their numbers back up. SNP were able to form a majority Government, an incredible feat under the 'Additional Member System' (AMS) proportional electoral system used to elect the Scottish Parliament.

As always, there are a range of factors involved in winning or losing an election. Labour's defeat was added to by the fact that they were still campaigning in the same way as they did under First Past the Post, targeting key winnable swing voters in swing seats and hoping to hold onto 'safe seats' with minimal input. They added no new votes. The SNP realised that something different was required and that there was no such thing as a safe seat in the Scottish Parliament anymore, and went all out for a cross country vote and particularly, to get previous Lib Dem voters to come to them. Their vote went up by 12.5 per cent across the country, enough to wipe out Labour in much of its heartland. Labour's inability to learn new tricks and the SNP's innovation in campaigning added to this 'earthquake' result, which facilitated a majority SNP Government and the Scottish independence referendum.

The AMS system means that votes in all places are now much more equal in value than under 'First Past the Post.' It should incentivise a move away from the old segmentation and targeting. While a better system is necessary, that alone is insufficient, as decades of neglect and a culture of not voting will take much more than just a different electoral system and a change in campaigning to fix. As stated earlier, the turnout in 2011 was only 52 per cent.

The experts

The world and its policy challenges have grown in complexity – from Cold War game theory to climate modelling and now, in Scotland in the year of the referendum, currency arrangements and the politics of austerity. What seems to be growing complexity must also mean a related growth in the importance of a question that had been around since the early part of the 20th century (Dewey 1927). If our society was so complex that it required to be run by experts, how did that reconcile itself with democracy? Citizens with apparently equal rights were conceding more power to 'super citizens' because of their expertise in science, economics or in government.

This requirement for experts and specialists has not only dominated our policy making at a national level, in all parts of society power and status has been given to professionals including lawyers, doctors, planners, environmental health officers, engineers and housing officers. This creation of a professional society has led to many important advances. Lawyers have helped develop and defend lots of political and social rights and freedoms, and the medical profession has helped most of us to live longer and for many ailments and diseases to be cured (Fischer 2009). Engineers and scientists have given us transport systems and communication networks that have connected us in ways we hardly imagined.

These successes led to huge amounts of public trust being invested in professionals, and with that trust came power. Decisions made on a 'professional' basis seem to be imbued with extra authority, and it can then be assumed that the 'correct' decision has been arrived at through the weighing up of carefully collected facts analysed by learned minds.

The experts' role became a matter for concern over the last few decades as it was understood and explained that experts were not always neutral bringers of information or knowledge. They also have values and even ideologies that they bring to the decision-making process. Citizens began to realise that they were not solely concerned with the public good and that many professionals have overtly turned to making money and maintaining and raising their own social status and power (Fischer 2009).

This is entwined with a cultural shift away from how society awarded status. As wealth and influence rose in public consciousness as things to be admired, public service declined in status. The idea that public service was a rewarding and valuable undertaking gave way to the idea that it might be subservient, wasteful and riding on the back of business. This made it easy to marketise and privatise, often on the advice and with support of professionals, and in some ways professionals were colluding in their own public decline as trusted public servants. However, the dominant cultural fashion for markets and business type success overruled more enduring principles, so is it surprising that wealth status and power overcame ethics? As happened with politicians, it is often the hypocrisy that erodes faith in these groups that leaves people feeling manipulated and misled.

Trust has fallen in the professional and the expert, although they are not as untrusted as the politician. There are still residual traditions of the professions being competent, dependable, accountable, trustworthy, loyal and honest. However, this positive view is increasingly in decline and they are often seen as arrogant, self-serving, exclusive and elitist (Berube 1996). Expertise is an additional source of legitimacy in public policy-making beyond electoral mandates. Individuals who have studied a policy area in detail and are recognised for it through professional bodies or academia are still given authority, especially if believed to be following an ethical code of conduct. Often politicians have relied on experts to increase their legitimacy, for example the Scottish Government established its Committee of Economic Advisors peopled by world leading economists to advise on its economic strategy and the possible design of a monetary and tax system should Scotland become independent.

While it might be said that the power of the expert is reined in by their accountability to democratically elected politicians, they are also often seen as using their authority and techniques to shore up and protect the political and economic elites. Professional experts have been portrayed by those who study such things as continuing, if not actually creating, some of the social injustices that we find impacting on the non-voter (Illich 1989). The greatest disappointment of the expert is that they have been unable to solve these social injustices and other big problems such as the degradation of our global environment and climate change.

Of course, people with in-depth understanding and knowledge of technical aspects of our world are valuable and, indeed, essential. However, as people come to see the limitations of the expert, there is growing real-isation that no decisions are purely technical – they are all made in social and community contexts. If these decisions are to involve values, then citizens have at least as much expertise as the professional, and when it comes to how their local community and economy functions, they are greater experts. To restore trust we must find a way to rehabilitate the professional expert with the citizens and to fuse their different types of expertise into democratic decision-making.

CHAPTER FIVE

Liar! Liar!

Irate Gentlemen: You are a fraud, a charlatan and a rogue, sir!

WC FIELDS: Ah – is that in my favour?

IF WE WERE to be truly honest about politics, we would admit that it is often a dishonest undertaking. The 19th-century Prussian military strategist Carl von Clausewitz said that, 'War is the continuation of politics by others means.' Modern politics is weighed down with military metaphor and language. Political campaigns are fought in 'war rooms' and in 'battlefield seats,' against 'enemies' with 'allies' using 'strategy' and 'tactics'. It is highly probable that a state of war from tribal skirmish to city state clashes was the long time predecessor of a state of modern politics, so that politics is rather the continuation of war by other means.

The ongoing Northern Ireland peace process shows us the need for politics. If different groups in society with conflicting interests are to argue out their difference without force of violence, then politics provides the means. It is not always high minded or elegant, but compared to bloodshed and bombing, its merits are obvious. It is the continuation of war by far kinder means. This is important, as we must understand why deceit and subterfuge are fundamental to politics. The key strategic decision of any General is to decide whether to use force or guile (Freedman 2013). This polarity of strategy in politics and in war is ancient. Homer described it as *bei* and *metis* (strength and cunning), personified respectively in Achilles and Odysseus. Over time this became 'force or guile,' as described by Machiavelli in the principle text on early statecraft, *The Prince*. In modern politics and in a democracy we hope to limit the use of force. That is one of the many successes of the system, but then, the only strategic option left is guile. This almost inevitably means misrepresentation, concealment and deception.

When the Coalition Government came to power, they made it clear they had no choice but to make drastic cuts in public spending, cuts that are hurting the young and the poor (see Table 15). Leading into the 2010 election and afterwards, George Osborne warned of a 'Greek-like Tragedy' if spending and debt were not cut hard and fast (Kirkup 2009). This was based on frightening stories of UK Government borrowing costing so much that mortgage rates would skyrocket and employment would tumble. This version of the situation is highly contested by many, including world leading economists such as Paul Krugman (Mooney 2013), who think that austerity and spending cuts actually caused the double dip recession; a position mostly endorsed by a contrite IMF when they admitted that the hard sums had been a bit beyond them and they had got it wrong on austerity (Schneider 2013).

Table 15 – Average annual real terms cuts in income or support by 2015

Groups defined by poverty indicators and benefit claimants	Most Citizens (not in other categories)	People in Poverty	Disabled People
Per person average annual real terms cuts in income or support by 2015	£546	£2,497	£3,973

Source: Cumulative Impact Assessment 14 November 2013

David Cameron, Nick Clegg and others have talked about the lack of alternatives to the cuts. In Cameron's 2010 New Year message he stated:

> I didn't come into politics to make cuts. Neither did Nick Clegg. But in the end politics is about national interest, not personal political agendas. We're tackling the deficit because we have to – not out of some ideological zeal. This is a Government led by people with a practical desire to sort out this country's problems, not by ideology.
>
> UK Government Speeches

However, in his speech to the Lord Mayors Banquet on 12 November 2013 in the City of London he said:

> We are sticking to the task. But that doesn't just mean making difficult decisions on public spending. It also means something more profound. It means building a leaner, more efficient state. We need to do more with less. Not just now, but permanently.
>
> UK Government Speeches

This all seem to point to one thing. The depth and speed of cuts were unnecessary. They were not the result of forces outside the control of Government, but were decision made by politicians because they fitted a certain set of interests and a particular view of the world. These policies benefitted one group and harmed another, with the group harmed the most being the ones not voting. So why did the Conservatives pretend that they were so heavily contained by capital flows and potential costs of borrowing that they had to make cuts that proved damaging to the economy? It seems unlikely that they deliberately harmed the economy, though it could be argued that they would have been more honest to say it was a price worth paying for a smaller state and more space for prof-it-making business.

This book is not about the highly technical debate of Keynesianism versus Austerity economics, but about why people feel disconnected from politics. If the people that took part in the focus groups in Dundee and Glasgow had heard anything of David Cameron's speeches it would be top line messages and they certainly would not have applied economic theory to any bit of it. But it is not unreasonable to assume that had they followed the narrative of austerity and cuts in any way, they might have felt angry. These cuts hurt them and others they knew. So why are they not determined to vote out the Tories as soon as possible? Perhaps what they got from this was not that they should vote out the Tories, but that politicians as a class are duplicitous and tricky. Perhaps they already know that this is not just a problem of the way the Tories do politics, but a problem with politics Per Se. It is not difficult to find examples of similar veneers of motivation given by politicians that seem to be used to hide or dissemble other reasons for doing things.

The currency argument

The issue of currency has become a major battleground in the Scottish referendum debate. Both campaigns and the parties for which the debates are often proxies have set out their positions on the matter of whether an independent Scotland can use the UK pound as its currency.

'If Scotland walks away from the UK, it walks away from the UK pound,' George Osborne UK Chancellor declared on 13 February 2014 on a trip to Edinburgh (Black and James 2013). This was one of a series of coordinated announcements from the three big UK parties around this time. Danny Alexander, Lib Dem First Secretary to the Treasury, and Alistair Darling, Labour Leader of the Better Together campaign, all said similar things. The message was clear and strong – under no circumstances would an independent Scotland be able to use sterling as its currency.

'Blocking an independent Scotland's ability to share the pound could damage business in the rest of the UK,' (Black & James 2013) said First Minster Alex Salmond on 17 February 2014. Again, this was one of a series of announcements both before and after UK parties announced their unequivocal position on the currency. The message was that the UK had little choice but to agree to a currency union with Scotland.

Detailed analysis of both these positions would on the whole conclude that they are conjecture and negotiating positions. Both sides have very much overstated their case to maximise what they think will be the political advantage, to 'scare' or 'allay the fears' of people. The Scottish Trades Union Congress (STUC) second status report on the nature of the referendum debate in late February 2014 summed up the position well:

> Whilst it is fair to say that there has been an increase in available information on offer from the respective governments, campaigns, political parties and the academic community, the presentation and commentary associated with this information still continues to frustrate reasoned debate. Whilst a significant proportion of Scottish voters state that they require additional information, an even greater proportion of voters state that they are finding it difficult to decide whether the information which they are being provided with is true or not.
>
> STUC 2014

Many people reading this will themselves have had the feeling that whether it is David Cameron on the economy, or Alex Salmond, George Osborne or Alistair Darling on a future Scottish currency, they are either telling us something not quite true or not telling us the whole story.

Seasoned commentators and diehard political hacks will know, understand and accept this behaviour, noting perhaps that this is just the cut and thrust of politics. Academics and scholars of history and strategy might even say that is inevitable. Politics is much preferable to war as a means of sorting out our differences, and as Machiavelli and many others tell us, without recourse to force, politics *is* the operation of guile. This is not to say that politics does not also have highly honourable aims. The objectives of making society better and allowing citizens to live a good life can be of high moral calling. However, if the way that politics has evolved and currently operates is through characteristics and behaviours of conceal-ment, deceit, trickery and surprise, then it is no wonder that many people find it distasteful and untrustworthy. These are ways of acting that are seen as, at best, amoral in a society with a Judeo-Christian heritage.

The tricks of the trade

Earlier it was shown how the rise of a professional class of politician narrowed representation and shut out other types of representative. Trained from an early age – probably starting by carving a route up through student politics, such a person then takes a job as an elected member's researcher or in a think tank – all the while learning how to craft a message or to spin a story. This monoculture has manufactured our political stars in the same way that *XFactor* makes pop stars. Such politicians know how to avoid answering a difficult question, how to wrong-foot their opponent, to run a rebuttal operation to refute anything bad said about them, and to then put out 'attack' lines and 'go negative' on an enemy.

Coming from the same backgrounds, using the same rhetorical tricks and trying to squeeze into a winning mould means politicians often sound the same. That same is a strained sincerity if they are good at it, or, if they are still learning, a dodgy salesman. Yet people now know the tricks of the trade because they read newspapers and watch TV and movies. All the pundits and commentators want to be seen as clever enough to be in on the 'dark arts', so they are discussed in broad daylight.

So what has changed? Was politics not ever thus? Of course partly it was. However, the greatest deceit of politics was to show the people its often honourable ends, and to conceal its dishonourable means, in order to pretend that it is better than it is. The aim was to project an image of an elite in order to justify *being* an elite, a political class who were better in expertise and in morals than the people. Most people can of course be guileful in their lives, but we're led, perhaps rightfully so, to expect better of our leaders. What has changed is that elites no longer universally control the flow or presentation of information. The people who took part in the focus groups would almost certainly struggle to demonstrate how and why they were being misled by politicians, but they knew that they were. Dorothy's dog, Toto, pulling away the curtain to expose the illusion that the 'Great Almighty Oz' is merely an old man and not a wizard is an overused metaphor to explain the dishonesty of power, but for the millions of people who do not vote, that curtain has fallen.

CHAPTER SIX

Understanding New Times

The windmill gives you society with the feudal lord: the steam-mill, society with the industrial capitalist.

KARL MARX

A different Scotland

IN DAVID ATTENBOROUGH'S BBC *Life on Earth* series, the final episode that sought to understand how human beings have come to dominate was entitled 'The Compulsive Communicator'. Our compulsion to find out and to tell about what we have found are drives that have always changed human society. The revolution in electronic communication was both a product of and facilitator of these compulsions, the same compulsions that drove people to share how to make fire and to describe the theory of relativity. Those of us who waste time on the internet or Twitter or Facebook are only too aware how basic this compulsion is. The materiality, practicalities and need for effort that previously constrained these drives have all but gone. Information was once held on material documents and could only be seen by those close by or reported on by those that had seen it. Knowing what was going on in millions of places and in millions of events was impossible to collect and store, share or analyse. It was hard to know how people who lived in different places and lived different lives thought and felt about the world, to know what motivated them or how they behaved – particularly those with the power to control the release and presentation of information. They could try to control how we saw them and how they were perceived, and of course, a massive industry and science grew up around that – that is the industry of public relations, an industry that both took from and lent to the political tricks of the trade.

Understanding the world and making judgements about it was difficult when most people could only see a tiny fragment of the picture. Those that could see more of this picture had a huge advantage: they had much more power. Maintaining scarcity of information and concentrating it within elites was the architecture of the old hierarchy. Tony Blair in his memoirs wrote that his greatest regret in Government was introducing the Freedom of Information Act (Pidd 2010). There are still crazy conspiracy theorists out there, but that does not mean that there are not real conspiracies to manipulate populations and to maintain power. Some would say the mask slipped when Blair expressed his biggest regret and maybe he thinks it better when only a few people have access to the bigger picture. That does not however take away from the fact that Blair wants to keep many things secret from the public. He may feel like a protective parent looking after naïve children, or he may want unfettered power to do what he thinks is best, but whatever his motivation, most people would not agree with him.

In his 1974 book, *Anarchy, State and Utopia*, Robert Nozic introduced a thought experiment he called the 'Experiential Machine' or 'Pleasure Machine' – the proposition was that if human brains could be connected to a machine that guaranteed a simulated lifetime of pleasure, would people eschew reality to take up the offer? It is safe to say that most would refuse the opportunity of a virtual reality despite it being less painful than reality, and this idea was reworked in the 1999 film *The Matrix*. This experiment demonstrates the innate human search for a reality, to see things as close as possible to how they really are. The fact that we choose reality over pleasure should tell Tony Blair that we want to know as much as possible about how we are governed and those that govern us; not a partial picture with parts withheld by those who think they know what is best. We are also of course very suspicious and untrusting when things are kept from us – 'Sunlight is the best disinfectant,' said Conservative Party leader David Cameron when praising the philosophy of WikiLeaks at a TED conference in 2010 (Hassan 2010).

Change in how information is collected, stored and shared has been revolutionary. This information revolution is multi-layered and not always easy to understand, because like all great paradigm shifts, it involves relationships between society and technology and the effect they have upon each other. Karl Marx is, not surprisingly, often mistaken for a prophet rather than a philosopher. His idea that the economic base gave rise to a social superstructure makes sense. To recall the quote at the beginning of this chapter, Marx wrote that 'the windmill gives you society with the feudal lord: the steam-mill, society with the industrial capitalist' (Engels and Marx 1847). We are starting to see the potential of what social media and smartphones might mean for a social order.

Technology changes people and people in turn change the world. Part of the challenge is not only that there always have been gatekeepers to information, but that the big picture has always been unimaginably big. Of course we cannot know the entire complexity of cause and effect, of relationships and motivations across our whole globe, but we can collect information about things that are going on in millions of places and analyse it and look for patterns in what has become known as big data. Instead of millions of pieces of paper or massive areas of expensive memory banks, big data is stored electronically in smaller and smaller spaces. To share big data in the past, it would have had to be copied on to paper and physically moved (assuming it was even possible to collect that data in the first place), but now we can download it from a server, send a link to a friend or thousands of people via social media. We can see more and more of the big picture, and this is having a profound effect on the power architecture of our society. Elites are no longer elite although they are of course still trying to be so. A society that is much flatter is a society made to be democratic. The problem may not be a crisis of democracy, but a crisis of too little democracy.

The institutions

To think about how power is exercised in Scotland we must look at the institutions, the structures that make things happen. They move information through media; money and capital through banks; provide services and infrastructure – both private and public – through government and corporations. This is the framework around which our society functions, and the decisions that are made mostly at the top of these organisations have big effects on the lives of Scots. They are the channels through which power flows, and in describing them below, it is in the context of the new times described above. This will show that they are possibly too slow to change to meet the new times, that they are a block on progress and a danger to democracy because their inability to stay relevant eats away at their legitimacy. They seem trapped in centralised 'verticalism' and in thrall to the expert.

The public services

People experience governments most vividly where they have contact with its services. It is not the upper chamber of the palace of Westminster or the Council of Ministers in Europe or even the Council Chamber of their so called 'local' government that gives them direct experience of government – it is having bins emptied, driving along roads or applying for social housing where the state and people meet. The big question is whether that is an empowering or disempowering experience, and in many cases it is the latter. Perhaps it must be that way. Collective provision means that there must be compromises, as not every service can be tailor made for each individual. There also must be a degree of rationing of public services, as not everyone can have what they want and if they did, some would always want more anyway.

Is this a reason for discontent and disengagement? People surely understand that public provision cannot be uniquely shaped for their needs, and to a large part accept that. That is not to say that one size fits all in a collective provision, and there are surely improvements that can be made in flexibility and towards more personal, or more local, shaping of services. Perhaps though, as many have suggested, this feeling of disempowerment comes from stuff being done to people all the time instead of stuff done with them. That is the very nature of disempowerment – things being done *to* you, alongside having no ownership, no control and also no responsibility.

The appearance of 'them and us' that has grown up between public services and the public is troubling. The ideal would be for the public to think of the local public services as providing services for 'us.' This concept appears much stronger in states of Northern Europe that have smaller and more local units of government. In Nordic countries the term 'Folkhemmet' is used to refer to what we call the Welfare State. The literal translation is 'the people's home,' which outlines a very different attitude to public provision than the one that has developed in Britain.

A recurring theme in political discussion is the lack of responsibility that citizens take for their own places or their own actions. Run down housing estates are often further blighted by the actions of their residents. Vandalism, littering and antisocial behaviour are all the things that make some places bad places to live. An interesting question is what comes first: the abdication of responsibility or the lack of power and ownership? There is no easy answer, as some people will behave badly and refuse to accept responsibility, will not care about where they live and how bad things are for them, let alone for their neighbours. It might be easy to say that some people are just born that way, but that would be largely untrue and lazy thinking. The tiny amount of people who are damagingly anti-social – and it is a tiny amount – have been socially engineered that way. Removed of status and power with limited resources to obtain any, this is what can happen to human beings. Not always but often when people are given power, some status and ownership, they accept responsibility. It would be interesting to see how far this reverse social engineering can work. It is certainly not a quick fix, but there are many reasons why it would be a worthwhile undertaking.

For generations, if not forever, it has been the nature of our institutions, of our managers and of our leadership for that accrual and centralisation of power to be socially incentivised. It is incentivised both through status and through financial rewards via pay. A public servant is typically paid more depending on how many people they manage and often over the size of geography they have responsibility for. This is incentivized disempowerment, as it takes power from people from local workers and from places.

Scottish local government

There are a growing number of voices that question the term Scottish local government. What do we mean by local? Legitimacy and trust tend to decline the more remote decisions are from the people, both in terms of geographical distance, but also distance from their 'lived life' experience. People like to feel that those making the decision have some shared interest and risks; ideally they will use the same facilities and services, and face the same problems they do. That is certainly more likely if they live in the same place. There are also questions of shared identity and a local unit of identity is important as a symbol of shared interests. So if people belong to the same town, village, housing scheme or estate, then that immediately communicates a likelihood of shared interest. Most local authorities in Scotland are too large to harness that connection of local identity where it is strongest. An example would be that most Fifers would identify as Fifers, but feel much more connected to their local town or village and would want people from there making as many decisions as possible – not a few from their local town diluted by a predominant number from the rest of Fife. People from Dunfermline want to run Dunfermline, for example.

A powerful argument for more local democracy is that people who live in the community will understand and talk about the place in which they live in a different way. Local citizens have a different cultural, historical and spatial understanding of their community and thus will make decisions about priorities or opportunities for that community with a different mindset from more remote decision makers. An additional benefit is that reconnecting with politics at a local level could help to open up participation at other levels.

Visibility and transparency usually increase with proximity. These are basic principles in which trust is built. It would be ideal if most people in a community knew, or knew people who knew, their local representative. This can only be achieved in much smaller units of governance. This must be balanced with systems and checks that guard against patronage, kin preference and nepotism. The best way to do this is to accept that this behaviour is innate and so assume it will always occur unless corrective measures are in place.

Holyrood

The Scottish Parliament has been in existence since 1999. Although very young in life as these things go, in that time it has grown in trust and stature. Its earliest years were marred by controversy and some almost snobbish disdain – probably fuelled by political briefings and manoeuvrings of Scottish MPs decidedly miffed at losing some of their power and the Scottish political media spotlight shifting away from them and to the work and personalities of Holyrood. The media was of course right to shift their gaze. The Scottish Parliament is closer and more relevant to the lives of Scots than Westminster could ever be. Over the years, trust and confidence in this institution has grown so that now most Scots would prefer it to be responsible for running all government departments, except for defence and foreign affairs – and that includes raising tax and allocating benefits. Its Proportional Electoral system, which gives seats to representatives in proportion to the votes that were cast for them, means Scotland's Parliament operates much more like the democracies of Northern Europe than the UK Parliament.

Many, particularly those outside the Central Belt, still feel that the Parliament is remote from them. The Parliament itself strives to develop its own culture and much of its literature and debates seem to refer to and recognise the assertion that in Scotland the people are sovereign. This is in marked contrast to Westminster where the concerns and calls to political arms, especially against Europe, are for defence of parliamentary sovereignty. That is not to say that the Scottish Parliament has not inherited some bad habits from its parent in London. Scotland had known a Westminster Parliament for hundreds of years and despite its horseshoe chamber and its proportional system of elections, the Westminster tradition of aggressive and confrontation political debate is thriving in the chamber at Holyrood. This is unfortunate, as this macho form of politics is an aspect of governance that ordinary people despise, generating a genuine factor in making them turn away from politics.

Most, but not all, parliaments in advanced liberal democracies have two chambers. Usually one is there to suggest legislation, and one to amend and improve proposed laws. This is seen as a way to make more considered laws and as a form of checks and balances on the power of the parliament and the government. The Scottish Parliament has only one chamber, and for those who shaped and put in place the workings of the new parliament, the reasoning was clear. This was to be a regional parliament, not a parliament of an independent state and did not require the same counter weights against the power of a government. The proportional electoral system was deemed to guarantee there would be no majority in the chamber and therefore the chambers itself could act as a check against the Government. However, in 2011 the SNP won a surprise majority and taught us all that what seemed impossible ten years before can become the accepted norm in a very short time. Maybe this demonstrates why some people defend constitutions that formed and have been tested over long periods of time, fearing the unpredictability of the future and the unintended consequences of change. The Scottish Parliament also has Westminster watching over it – in theory, at least, that parliament remained sovereign with control over the economy, defence and welfare and ultimately the power to abolish the Scottish Parliament. While legally feasible, it is politically impossible. So without a second chamber, Holyrood uses a system of committees to provide scrutiny of and to make amendments to Scottish legislation as it makes its way through the Parliament.

Westminster

Westminster considers itself the mother of all parliaments, and the palace of Westminster has been the centre of power for England and then the UK for over 900 years. It has not been a seat of representative democracy for most of that time. Up until 1918, nearly 60 per cent of men were excluded from voting due to property qualifications and it was only the immense sacrifice made by the working classes in the First World War that meant their exclusion from the franchise became indefensible, even to the British elites. 1918 was not particularly early for universal male suffrage, as most European states had granted this sometime before, but woman had to wait until May 1929 before they were able to exercise equal voting rights, in the so-called flapper election.

Unlike the Scottish Parliament, the British Parliament has a second chamber – the House of Lords. The House of Lords Act, brought in by Tony Blair's first Government, reformed the chamber in 1999, expelling the majority of the house who were still hereditary peers (661). These were men (and it was mainly men, as titles are inherited through the male line) who were part of the UK Parliament by merit of birth. A deal was struck at that time to allow 92 hereditary Lords and the Lords Spiritual (22 Bishops) to remain until the second phase of reforms. That has yet to happen and the Lords now is peopled by Bishops, Hereditaries and Life Peers, or those appointed by the Government of the day. Not a single member of the British Parliament's second chamber is elected by popular vote of the people. While much of this is history, it is important history, as it affects the current culture and values of the place, and it meant that when the Liberal Democrat part of the Coalition Government sought to reform the Lords to have an elected element, the Tory party and parts of the Labour Party kicked it out.

The chamber that seems democratic, the House of Commons, is elected by what many consider an out-dated electoral system. First Past the Post may have worked fairly well when the vast majority of the electorate voted either Conservative or Labour, but with SNP, Lib Dems, Greens and now UKIP in the calculations, the system returns results that fail to reflect the wishes of the voters. With the electorate split between so many options, it turns out that many MPs had more people voting against them than for them. In 2010, what was once a two-party system creaked and cracked as the voters delivered a hung parliament. Many are aware that due to concentrations of particular types of voters in particular areas, their votes will never really count. Scotland is still significantly overseen by the most centralised government in Europe, led by a Conservative party that holds only one Westminster seat in Scotland, but this is of course softened by the fact that we have our own Parliament elected by PR. However, it feels strange, perhaps because it highlights the clash of centralised, vertical, top-down authorities with a modern world of self-directed networks and horizontal relationships.

The democratic deficit at Westminster has actually decreased over the last 20 years, particularly in relation to the Lords with the removal of most of the birth right peers. Most MPs will tell you they work harder in their constituency and do more surgeries and case work than they have ever done before. Things might have carried on quite happily as they had before, with MPs working harder and harder to stem a steady but slow erosion of their status and therefore their power, if not for one momentous moment in British political history. A moment that showed why information and the way it can be stored and shared might change the power relationships of states and citizens forever. That moment was the MP expenses crisis. In 2009, before Parliament could comply with a High Court ruling upholding a Freedom of Information request to release details of MPs' expense claims, it was leaked to the *Daily Telegraph*. Moat cleaning and duck houses paid for by the public purse convulsed the political order and an already declining sense of trust and deference nosedived and has never come back up. The Hansard Society's annual audit of UK political engagement in 2013 found that people thought things were only getting worse, with only 23 per cent of people saying they are satisfied 'with the way MPs in general are doing their job', the lowest level ever recorded in the Audit series. Worryingly for MPs, satisfaction levels are now six per cent lower than they were three years ago, following the parliamentary expenses scandal. Interestingly, fewer people are dissatisfied with MPs (38 per cent compared to 44 per cent), as an increasing proportion of people are 'neither satisfied not dissatisfied' (37 per cent, up from 24 per cent three years ago) – in other words, a rising tide of simply not being interested.

Brussels

Politicians are sensitive to power. It's a form of nutrient that they can feel when it's filling them up or when it's ebbing away. And as it drains away from Westminster, MPs are frantically searching around to see who is stealing it. Someone else must be to blame, as it certainly cannot be anything that they have done. That power is seeping away from MPs is true. The why, the how and the where is not simple, but for many unlikely to see the nuances, Brussels and the EU are too big to miss. If it wasn't for Tory guns trained on Europe, most citizens would be unlikely to know that the EU has a role in governing us – it is, after all, further away than Edinburgh and even further than London. The EU does affect the way Scotland is run and probably affects our lives every day. In Scotland the EU would appear not to be such a bogey man, perhaps because those inclined that way have enough to shake their fist at with Westminster, or perhaps it is just because there are less Tories.

The EU in many ways is a fantastic achievement; many Europhile Leaders of European states will tell us that it is the harbinger of the longest peace Europe has ever known. The relative harmony, integration and unity must be acknowledged and admired. The truth too is that some elements of the European social model have been transmitted to Scottish lives through rules and laws that have been handed down from the EU, such as workers' protection and guaranteed holidays. There are many buts, though. The term 'democratic deficit' was coined in relation to the EU. The workings of the European Commission, the Parliament and its other organs are anything but transparent and not because they necessarily seek to be secretive. However, place and proximity comes into play once again. The EU may be a community of sorts for the politicians, the leaders and the autocrats, but it is not a community that the vast majority of Scots really feel they belong to. It is just impossible to feel relevant as an individual in a community of millions of people.

These challenges of geography and scale have been made worse by the Euro Crisis. *The Economist* Index of Democracy notes a significant decline in democracy across Europe with the democratically elected governments of Greece then Italy, Portugal and Ireland either temporarily replaced or heavily leaned on by the bankers of the European Central Bank and the big politicians of the bigger states predominately Germany.

Political parties

The days of mass membership political parties are long gone. Political party membership is at a historic low, with SNP in Scotland and UKIP in England being notable exceptions. There are specific circumstances that account for the growth of SNP; part of it is about defections from Labour as the realignment of New Labour opened up recruiting ground for SNP left of centre. The Scottish independence referendum was also a chance for SNP to add members. Campaigning for that referendum promises an outcome beyond traditional politics, and for some it is an anti-establishment activity.

This also highlights the success of UKIP. UKIP are an indication of disaffection with political parties. The continuing decline of political parties is not difficult to understand when looking at the earlier parts of this book and the Scottish Labour Party are a case in point. Under Tony Blair, the victory of the Leaders office over the other centres of power (Conference and the National Executive Council) for control of the party was total. This meant that Labour rapidly centralised and became more top-down as society began to gradually move the other way. Doubly damaging for Scottish Labour was that this centralisation was in London, and Scottish Labour seemed to have a policy agenda for the South of England as a newly devolved Scotland started to change. Their local structures have slowly declined, hastened by changes in the industrial base and unions as well as losing councillors to a change in the electoral system and falling levels of social housing tenants due to Right to Buy (Hassan and Shaw 2012).

The rise and stagnation of the institutions

Centralisation of power happens in local government, it happens in central government departments, it happens in commerce and business, in banks and corporations, in the BBC and in the trade unions. It has been happening for centuries and is now one of the dominant effects of progress. It is driven by a range of factors and in early 21st-century Scotland it is both a result of a certain set of values and a perpetuator of those values. These are values that, while often claiming to support individual freedom and choice, predominantly expect that individual freedom and choice to be expressed in terms of accrual of power and wealth. That has meant larger institutions, competitions won and lost for control of those institutions, mergers and take overs, and almost as an unintended consequences of this, people are smaller and smaller in relation to these institutions. This is not a removal of power once had or of the loss of a golden age, but it is a buffer to moving on to a flatter, more democratic model more in tune with our time. It is the institutional structure and values that block us from moving on to something better. It is the faltering and halting of increases in freedom and democracy. That halt in itself is of great concern because it stops Scottish society reaching its full potential, but we also know from history that when civilisation is halted it is often the conditions for decline. The opposite of growth is not stasis, but dieback.

Of course, power has traditionally been held in a concentrated centre. In an earlier search for the legitimacy of rulers, it was often stated and believed throughout medieval Europe that all power came from God and that one person – the Pope, King or Queen – was their representative on Earth. This idea is said to develop from Roman law and of course supported and spread by many self-interested monarchs across Europe. But it was James the VI and I who most exactly wrote about and explained it, both in a book on political theory, *The True Law of Free Monarchies*, and in his manual on government, the *Basilikon Doron* (or Royal Gift), addressed to his son but later selling thousands of copies that described the Divine Right of Kings as being like the duty of obedience that a child owed to his father. This concept of a paternal source of power is still important today in how we relate to and accept power – as children to a parent.

Accepting that others might know better than ourselves is often a useful act of humility. But it can also be an abdication of responsibility, a more comfortable and easy option. If someone wants to make the decisions for us and take the flack if things go wrong, then many of us will stand aside and let them. Particularly if we think, perhaps with good reason, that they will achieve better outcomes for us. Here is a construct to help us think about this problem.

This disempowerment is a two-way street. There are those who want power as an end in itself or because they know how to utilise it in their interests or in the interests of those they wish to serve. Let's call these the 'power seekers' and it is true that many power seekers who enter politics and sometimes other spheres are motivated at least in part by public interest. It is also true that it is not easy for power seekers to separate out their own personal desire for power and the public interest motivation for power, and this is particularly true when the personal and social rewards of power have been experienced including status, obedience, wealth and security. As mentioned above, there are also those who give away their power, it seems willingly, and who can be termed 'power fearers'. Is this sort of submissive characteristic something for which they should be blamed? Or is it inevitable that large parts of the Scottish population behave like this when faced with the current configurations of power and the institutions that administer it?

This seems like a rock and a hard place. The building of institutions, and the way they are set up is in itself sucking away power from people who feel they have no real say in how they shape their lives. Their wages are falling, housing is bad or there is not enough of it or it is too expensive. The safety net of the Welfare State is under attack. This was not so alienating when there was residual faith that the people running government, banks and local authorities were acting in their own interests perhaps, but those interests often coincided with the peoples. Our leaders were all trying their best for us, but although it was all just too difficult, trust remained – it was weak, but it was there.

For these reasons, people no longer trust these institutions, as it was found that they were trying their best for themselves often while hurting us. If people want these institutions to act in the public interest, they must find ways to take back their power and to exert new authority over them. This is extremely difficult, and the resources and conflict that might arise from trying to take power back is perhaps seen as too costly. The population's reaction to what seems like an impossible task is to become entirely alienated, and then the whole exercise of democracy becomes pointless. The Police, the BBC, politics, banks, the media and organised religion are the places losing trust, legitimacy, and therefore power. A growing number of people are turning their back on even attempting to hold our institutions to account through the ballot box. Why waste your time on something that doesn't seem to work anymore? Those that run the institutions might momentarily rejoice in being free from democratic accountability. They should be careful what they wish for.

The perfect quiet storm

The 'missing Scotland' and the missing million are important, not only because they might decide the outcome of Scotland's independence referendum, but because they are one of the few quantifiable parts of a much bigger crisis. They are a bellwether, a symptom of something going wrong. The democratic theory goes that if a group of voters don't like what's happening to them, if their institutions fail them, their living standards fall, their communities – indeed their very culture – is harmed, then they will vote against the government. However, it seems that having tried voting with little success, this group have given up on it.

They no longer feel anyone is standing up for their interest. They are being left further and further behind and feel manipulated and lied to. The institutions that used to belong to and give them collective power have either been destroyed, declined or been taken over by people who are not like them. From banks to the BBC, people no longer believe in institutions that they used to trust to act fairly and in the interests of justice.

This was all manageable when elites controlled the dissemination and presentation of information. It is hard to know whether the age of deference was built on a time of real honour and public service or whether this was an illusion created by those in power. We looked up to our leaders and the experts, they knew better than us and were acting in all our interests, but free-flowing information has blown apart that myth. Those that seek power are much like the rest of us, flawed and defective, and maybe worse because they pretended they were better than us. George Osborne can make a speech about the overwhelming need for austerity in the morning and a video clip of Paul Krugman, Noble Prize winning economist, saying that he is talking nonsense can be seen by tens of thousands on social media by the afternoon.

Democracy is in a semi-permanent state of crisis. Its abiding strength is that its flexibility and adaptability mean that its failure usually becomes its success (Runciman 2014). Our ability to recognise and react to the failures keeps it evolving and rejuvenates the system whenever required. The big concern is that after centuries of this success, we might become complacent and expect someone else or the system itself to sort it and before we realise it, it's too late. This is David Runcimans 'Confidence Trap' (Runciman 2014).

It seems unlikely that we would fall into this 'Confidence Trap' at a time of war, or the massive financial crash of 2008, which we are still feeling the effects of in 2014. These are obvious crises that rally governments and people to action. The biggest threat, then, might be when we have a quiet crisis, one that grows over time so that necessary changes to the status quo are resisted by those who benefit from current arrangements. It grows, and then combines with, other subtle waves of shift and change until together they break over us – and we never even saw it coming. Strong metaphors, you might think, but the rise of right-wing anti-establishment parties across Europe has to be reckoned with – Le Pen in France, UKIP here and the Geert Wilders' Party for Freedom in Holland.

Benefit sanctions hitting poor people across the UK have left them feeling that they have little left to lose. This has consequences and implications. The Mayor of London, Boris Johnson, asked the Home Secretary in March 2014 to support the purchase and authorised use of water cannon by the Metropolitan Police Force of London (Crerar 2014). If granted, this will be the first time their use has been authorised on the UK mainland. What is he worried about?

CHAPTER SEVEN

From Failure to Success?

HUGE GAINS IN SOCIAL and economic equality in the last century were not, as some would tell us, brought about only by market innovation. More importantly was the success of representative democracy in being able to grant the poorer classes power through the trade unions and then through the Labour Party. The forces of technology and innovation could then be shaped somewhat in their interest as well. Technological changes overtook them and in a post-industrial world the institutions either declined, or could only adapt away from them and leave them behind. Local government, trade unions and the old Labour Party either represented others or lost power. This was a downward spiral of impotence as the 'missing voters' lost trust in what was left and stopped voting.

Rises in inequality are a symptom of the interplay between a political situation and the economic one. Those left behind no longer have any political power to shape the forces that make up our economy. The trick for democrats is to be pessimistic enough to see the crisis, but optimistic enough to see the opportunity for improvement. Antonio Gramsci sums this up well as 'pessimism of the intellect and optimism of the will' (Gramsci 1929).

The opportunity

The technological changes that first changed industry are changing politics. The information revolution makes us all much more equal in access to information and potentially more democratic as we can all access information that was once difficult to find. People other than media owners and journalists can present that information through all forms of media in pictures, video or text. Information is the fuel of decision-making: if ordinary people have access to more information the least they will know is that the experts and their leaders are not really solving the big problems. If we think that all Scots are of equal value and that our society should respect that principle, from that it follows that they deserve their fair share of power. The opportunity to achieve this has never been greater.

The ends of greater democracy and increased equality are for the first time in history also the means.

The cause of human equality has moved forward – sometimes grindingly slowly, but at other times in what seem like great leaps. The spread of the franchise. Beveridge's innovations in health, welfare and housing, and the post-1945 Labour Government. Equality legislation in the 1960s and 1970s, and now equal marriage. Increases in workers' rights, first won by the trade unions and then through the EU. The Minimum Wage. Every one of these leaps was only possible because the slow grinding of the other times, when arguments and organisation were being built. All these big changes came through getting control of the levers of power and making sure there was enough space and support to pull them. The institutions and structures that achieved these things were, perhaps by necessity, hierarchical; after all, the state from the days of 'the divine right of kings' had been configured in such a way. Trade unions, political parties and local authorities were best to reflect this structure in order to engage with it. Because ultimately it was the state that made the laws and influenced the information flow that drove these changes. It may have been necessary, but for those who rose to power through such institutions, it was also desirable. Those that ran the trade unions in the 1960s and 1970s enjoyed the personal power as much as those who ran the banks in the 1980s and 1990s, although with more of a democratic leash. Whether banks or trade unions, these old vertical models no longer work on their own, and concentration of power – as it inevitably does – has corroded them from within. That corrosion began to be glimpsed and is now glaringly obvious for most to see, as the failure of the institutions becomes critical.

So the hierarchies in these institutions were also their limitation, as power held by a few meant power lost to the many. The advances through these structures have largely been halted, and the neo-liberal backlash of the last 30 years have meant that the new institutions of power that favour the few, not the many, have grown up. Sixty of the world's 100 largest economies are not states but corporations; so partly because democratic power is usurped from above, it is rejected from below.

The dangers here are manifold. In a Scotland without elites, many people would feel lost. We have been infantilised by relying on our leaders to tell us what to do and where to go, and the world will be a scary place to many, as that authority and those authority figures are lost. We have to grow up quickly and take responsibility for ourselves, but more importantly, for each other. That fear and anxiety is of course open to exploitation, and we can see the rise in populism across Europe and no less so in the UK. Populism is often wrongly understood to mean political policies that are popular in that they appeal to the 'populis'. In fact, in its strict usage it means dividing the population in two and turning a majority against a minority as a deliberate political strategy. A good example of this is the 'scroungers versus skivers' narrative, in which working people are turned against those on benefits, or the attempts to fuel resentment against immigrants by UKIP and elements of the Conservative Party. The classic divide and rule.

The rise of UKIP has much to tell us about some of those left behind by British politics. Matthew Goodwin, co-author of *The Revolution on the Right*, was quoted in a press release on the publication of the book in March 2014:

> UKIP are winning over the 'Left Behind' groups in British society: old, working class, men with very few educational qualifications. These are voters who hold a very different set of values to the professional, middle-class majority: they are far more nationalist, Eurosceptic, fiercely opposed to immigration and feel like they have no voice in politics. They look out at a country they neither recognise nor want to be a part of.

These are the very people that feel worried and scared by changes to our society, and the concern is that rather than bring about the radical evolution that is required to reinvigorate democracy, the current elite stand brittle against change and, when it comes, rather than renew our democracy, change might break it.

The rise of UKIP is so far a predominantly English insurgence. This is probably because the party activists and organisers are made up of disaffected Conservatives, often ex-councillors, although this is not necessarily where their votes come from. In Scotland there is not a disillusioned Tory infrastructure for UKIP to occupy. The focus group and survey work suggest that a party of the right, no matter how anti-establishment, might find it difficult to circumvent the deeply ingrained, leftist, working-class culture of the non-voting Scots, although gaining a Scottish seat in the 2014 Euro elections shows that Scots are not immune to their appeal. UKIP may be a protest vote but there are an awful lot of people who feel they have something to protest about.

The threat of authoritarian populism is real and present, and something to be watched for and guarded against. So are there other, better ways to progress that evolve with and bend to the people?

New ways of communicating and sharing information and disillusionment with the old have started to allow new forms of institution and organisation to form. In the UK, through groups like 38 degrees and Occupy, we get an idea of what a different, more democratic politics could look like. The old power architecture could facilitate this evolution in two ways. One would be negative, oppressive and potentially destructive. The knee jerk reaction might be to clamp down on these new horizontal forms of politics, and to think that the old parties and ways of government have a monopoly on politics. The recent so-called gagging law introduced by the UK Government to tightly control 'third party' campaigning in election years puts strict reporting and financial controls on organisations outside of political parties when campaigning for their concerns during elections. It particularly restricts organisations from forming coalitions to campaign, which is a fundamental characteristic of the horizontal politics. This is dangerous because if people have founds ways to express their political will within the democratic system of elections, but are oppressed in doing so, these energies and frustrations will find other outlets.

The second way that the existing system could facilitate the new horizontalism is by creating the political spaces and pathways for it to connect, work with and rejuvenate the old vertical politics. Falling turnout shows declining trust, the democratic state is in trouble. It is bleeding legitimacy and in its current configuration, it cannot solve big complex issues, such as inequality and climate change. Its failure could of course be the failure of democracy, so it is vital that we can turn this failure into success.

Running local places

A lot of people in Scotland have no daily contact with democracy; they have no contact in their immediate personal environment with democracy. That is not just a jigsaw piece that is missing in Scottish democracy; it is a founding stone of democracy that is missing in Scotland (participant in Electoral Reform Society, Democracy Max Peoples Gathering)

We have seen that exclusive power may not only operate centrally, and experts and professionals can have undue influence away from centres of power as well. Most political executive power is held centrally and the professions also tend to be part of a hierarchy. Hierarchies concentrate power at the top in the hands of a few people where big strategic decisions are made. The universities and professional bodes and regulators who influence the professions normally congregate as part of an upper tier and in a central place around the legislators and government. That top is a relatively small elite and has to be located somewhere. There are beneficial (to them) networks, meetings and discussions between those elites, and for these and other reasons, that place becomes the capital. That place might be Edinburgh or London, or it may be the largest town in the local government area, so Glenrothes is the administrative capital of Fife. A vertical elite-driven system inevitably concentrates power.

It seems clear that this concentration of power at the top and in the centre must be changed if people are to become re-engaged with democracy. They have realised that power is remote from them. That may have brought some advantages in the past and there are many elements of planning and statecraft that need to remain centralised. There are however a substantial and growing group of people who think that their interests are bypassed, and that they no longer have genuine representation as a direct consequence of hierarchy and centralisation.

The solution then is to share power downwards and outwards. There are many decisions that do not need to be made in Edinburgh or at local government level. Scotland has no real local government though, as the populations and size of areas that local administrations operate would, in most other European States, be considered Regional Government at a tier above the local (Bort, McAlpine and Mort 2012).

Legitimacy and trust tend to decline the more remote decisions are from the majority of people – both in terms of geographical distance from them but also in terms of relevance to their 'lived life' experience. People like to feel that those making the decision have some shared 'skin in the game,' as discussed earlier. That is certainly more likely if they live in the same place. Local citizens have a different cultural, historical and spatial understanding of their community and thus will make decisions about priorities or opportunities for that community with a different mindset from more remote decision makers.

Visibility and transparency usually increase with proximity. We can see and question the people involved, and perhaps the proceedings are observable. Visibility and transparency are basic elements on which trust is built, and what is not seen is hidden. An additional benefit is that reconnecting with politics at a local level could help to open up participation at other levels.

Different ways of deciding

The conflict model of Scottish politics is shaped by a powerful mix of history, structure and culture. Our history means that politics is, in some overall way, the continuation of war and conflict by non-violent means. This is true to a lesser or greater extent of all elite political systems, perhaps because the initial creation of states is a function of human conflict. Now we have arrived at a system with political parties with competing ideas of how to govern, but just as importantly with individuals and leaders who seek personal power and are vying to defeat each other.

The 'two tribes' Westminster structure reinforces this culture of conflict as well as the segmentation and targeting of some voters to the exclusion of others. In Scottish Parliament elections and Scotland's council elections, we are more like other European states in using proportional systems. This can indeed lead to a more collegiate and consensus type of politics in other states. However, generations of First Past the Post politics will take a long time to wash through the system, especially as a bipolar battle over independence has been the legacy of that system, and had the parties not been intent on defeating each other, a third option of so-called democracy max may have been on the ballot paper. This might have offered a unifying position with a significant majority of Scottish people in support, but instead the one question referendum has proven to be highly divisive and fraught with angry conflict.

Of course, political differences are fought over, and politicking is much preferred to violence, but surely we want more than just non-violent but sclerotic democracy? The truth is that this predominance of conflict and 'winner takes all' politics alienates many, and inevitably leads to the dishonesty that turns away voters and undermines democratic legitimacy. It is true that politics has been about contested ground because it has mostly been about contests over power at the top of the pyramid. Horizontal politics does not seem to present the same problems. Politics that might reflect our emerging society, as it in turn reflects the technological changes that have flattened it. We should explore ways to devolve power downwards and then outwards so that people can work together to make decisions and run their communities.

This needs to be a lot more comprehensive than just creating more mini parliaments and council chambers at more local level. Those systems of parties and representatives 'dividing' by vote on decisions, debating in ways that misrepresent others and misrepresent themselves, is just more of the same but with the advantage of being close to people and easier to watch. That is not to say that we do not need representative democracy, just that it needs to evolve to work with other ways of making decisions. Not only because those ways have lots to offer in making better decisions, but also because if they allow us to rely less on hierarchy and the inevitable elites and centralisation, we escape the conflict model and open politics up to honesty. Moreover, we allow people who are like the people who live in local places to make the decisions, meaning that we have government of the people by the people for the people.

One of the more participatory techniques of democracy that might strengthen and enhance representative democracy is Mini-publics. Mini-publics came about as a potential method of engagement that recognises the need for institutional reform, if people are to see the value of being involved in running their own communities. Mini-publics were proposed decades ago by political scientist Robert Dahl, who wondered whether we could envision a kind of mini-populis, representative of the population and empowered to learn about and deliberate on public issues, who would contribute directly to decision-making.

Mini-publics are designed to avoid the trappings of party politics and technocratic policy-making, and there are now an interesting variety of forms – each designed to work best for different purposes. From the now classic Citizens' Jury to the German Planning Cell, the Danish Consensus Conference or the Citizen Assemblies in Canada or Iceland, mini-publics are formed by randomly selected citizens (for instance, selected by lot from the electoral roll), usually to be representative of certain social characteristics, e.g. gender, age, ethnicity, that reflect the wider public. Mini-publics are empowered to call in a wide range of 'witnesses' to provide evidence and arguments on a given issue: officials, citizens, community activists, politicians, representatives from the third sector, businesses and academics. Finally, the mini-public deliberates on the evidence before reaching a recommendation or decision (Escobar 2013).

Reform of structures and institutions

We have seen how the nature of our institutions and power politics means that if there is nothing to stop it, then power will eventually move upwards. In Scotland, the Scottish Parliament can legislate in any way it likes over local government and we have seen an ongoing shrinking of local authority influence, particularly with controls on funding. This is almost inevitable in the current set up. The relationship between Westminster and the Scottish Parliament shows that where powers are protected by legislation, political legitimacy can grow so that this also becomes part of the protection. Westminster cannot interfere in Scottish health policy, for example, and while Westminster can legislate to change anything to do with the Parliament's power, if it has done so it has been to increase its powers. This is interesting and unusual because it is a downward flow of power. It is probably possible due to the equal mandate that they both have and the growing legitimacy of the Scottish Parliament. Support for the SNP has also given a political counterweight to Westminster, but it is true that even with a Labour government in Holyrood, that set of politicians would want more power, not less, and if they can 'punch at the same weight' then power won't be sucked upwards. While Westminster felt like it had primacy in the early days, they now feel more equal and people would prefer most government functions to be run from Edinburgh rather than London. Tightening the flow of money is one way that Westminster could have exerted more control over the Scottish Parliament but the exactness of the Barnett formulae and the threat of Scottish independence has managed to steady the hands on that lever. Watch this space if there is a significant No vote.

As has been said above, Scotland's current local government structure is really regional government. It is too remote from people and does not harness local identity. There needs to be a much lower level where communities can self-identify. We should think about turning the whole hierarchy on its head so that communities and local structures are at the top for many functions and central government below providing services to them. These small units can combine together to make larger units but always representing their communities.

If power is to be devolved further down to local communities, then similar sorts of political and legislative counterweights are required that enabled the Scottish Parliament to flourish. The SNP's promise to protect local government in a constitution is needed, but it needs to enshrine something more, such as 'every community to have a right to set up some form of governance' within the national framework and to raise revenues or have assets of some sort. If local people are truly involved in decision-making, and perhaps in creating services together through some of the techniques and innovations described here, then community units of government might attract the level of legitimacy and therefore political clout to be able to protect their own powers eventually. It is unlikely this legitimacy will arrive before legislation, just as it did not for the Scottish Parliament.

It must also be said that Westminster's antiquated ways are a serious threat to democratic legitimacy. The narrow representation is part of the problem. Add this to an unelected House of Lords and a Commons elected on an out-dated, divisive electoral system that forces politicians to ignore huge parts of the population. MPs attempts to reform themselves quickly enough have continually failed. Let's hope the politicians there are not caught in David Runciman's 'Confidence Trap.'

The new representatives

The Scottish Labour Party Conference 2014 in Perth was in many ways a showcase of all that is out of touch about politics, with a party that used to hold such unassailable sway over most of the Scottish population claiming again its right to govern. Speeches from the platform attacking the hated enemy, over-claiming what Labour were and could do and over denigrating the SNP, making a combination of hyperbole and spin that reinforced the systemic dishonesty of modern politics.

The hierarchy and status politics was not only obvious, but actively created and manipulated as it always had been, all in the cause of reaffirming power, with high stages and sets raising the select few into the spotlight. The leaders made big set-piece speeches; they told the audience how great they all were. This is the politics of big people leading; it is the politics of an elite at the top of a hierarchy. This is how it has been done for years, perhaps reaching its zenith in the great conference speeches of Tony Blair. The SNP conference is no different, and this is the way we have done politics for so long now, that the political class finds it hard to imagine anything else.

But Scottish Labour's 2014 conference was remarkable not only for its showcase of the old and out of touch, but also for a small but bright light of potential. A light that reaffirmed that democracy can turn failure into success. A young MSP, the Labour Spokesperson on Young People, gave up her opportunity to have centre stage and beguile the faithful from a podium. Instead, Kezia Dugdale, a representative for the Lothians, addressed a key referendum issue of childcare policy by inviting two mothers to the stage to speak about their experience of managing childcare for their own kids. Neither were members of the Labour Party and they were there as experts of their own experience.

In this relatively simple change of format, Ms Dugdale highlighted what could change if representative democracy is to make the space for other forms to fill the cracks and stabilise it once again. She demonstrated a different role for the representative one of giving opportunities for other voices to be heard, not voices who were experts through study or qualification, not professionals who might seek to argue for status or powers sake, but experts of a lived life experience. Their motives were clear – they wanted a better childcare system. These people were not members of the Labour Party and so did not have the organisation, its elites or hierarchies to impress or promote. They were not members of that tribe, but the tribe had been open enough (prised open perhaps by the young MSP) to hear their voices.

There are of course other 'New Representatives' in other parties and outside of parties – members of civil society, campaign groups, and community organisations. Democracy needs leaders but not like the old leaders. They were single minded, arrogant, driven, exclusive, heroic in an old fashioned way. The new leaders must be different; open minded, collaborative, listening, humble and inclusive. This role of the new representative, a role of facilitating all voices and of bearing witness to the lives of people means giving away power, sharing it downwards and outwards and leaving lots of room for horizontal movements, campaigns and structures to engage with the vertical.

The time of political monopolies and cartels should be passed. It is not a choice between one thing or another; between representative democracy or participative, horizontal or vertical, expert or citizen, local or national. Now is a time to make these things work together. New representatives and leaders, different, more inclusive decision making and real local power working together could help bring back the missing million and revert the democratic crisis. More than this: with their help, we can focus on representing their interests against the interests of an elite. Power and resources moved in that direction might ensure we have enough affordable homes, well paid and secure jobs and a new, open, less anxious, democratic Scotland.

The long term impact: challenging elite-run Scotland

Those dark winter evenings in Dundee and Glasgow when the focus groups met to provide the basis for this book could be seen as depressing portents for Scottish democracy. Digging deeper into what those people told us shows that what seemed on the surface to be the self-removal of a whole section of the population from the working of our democracy is in fact a systemic exclusion.

It is systemic because we have a political system that values conflict, scarcity and the dominance of one set of interests over another. This system has been so completely captured by the middle and managerial classes that they continue to entrench that power and whether deliberate or not kick down on those that have none. The alienation seems so complete that for the 'missing Scotland' voting in a general election seems as relevant as casting a vote for an election in some distant land.

The growing irrelevance of traditional forms of hierarchy and the new times we find ourselves driven by the rapid technological changes are happening across the world. They have produced far-reaching transformation and change at a pace difficult for many to comprehend. Here in Scotland we find ourselves in a particularly volatile political moment. Not only do we have the technological and social shake out happening but we also have the referendum on independence providing an opportunity for these new times to break through more obviously into one big political event.

The changes that are required to revitalise our democracy that are glimpsed at in the section above seem to be demonstrated in the Scottish referendum campaign. It would be partisan not to acknowledge that they are only being significantly demonstrated as part of the Yes campaign. This is obviously because the No campaign despite its attempts to frame itself as a campaign for a vote for change (only slightly less change) is inevitably a creation of the status quo.

It is the old way and an old form of politics. In a society that has too much fear already it seeks to add to the sum of that anxiety. They seek to achieve their objective, the maintenance of the British state in its current configuration by making people afraid of change. Fear of course can be a healthy emotion. We may well behave recklessly and self-harming without a healthy dose of fear. However, used instrumentally as a political tool it makes Scotland worse not better. It is almost always disempowering, for anxiety itself is a lack of power. Anxiety stems from a feeling of lack of control in what might happen to us. Will we keep our jobs, or have a house be able to pay the bills? Insecurity is the effect of these changing times but it has also been amplified as a political tool by all those who use it. It takes power away from people and seeks to concentrate it in the hands of the 'meaning makers' and the meaning they continue to make is a frightening one.

The Yes campaign are of course not above manipulating our emotions for political objectives, however the political forms and actions that has developed on the fringes of the Yes campaign look more like the fresh new ways that are necessary for these times.

National Collective, the Radical Independence Campaign, Common Weal, Bella Caledonia and many more local under-the-radar groups, groups that are self-organised and crowd-financed through online donations and memberships – these groups sit outside the traditional political setup, yet it can be argued have had a growing influence on the feel and framing of the debate. Presenting Yes as much more than an elite project while helping to back No into that 'top down' corner.

The effect of this on voters may be significant. Studies of change referendums across the world suggest that 'No change' is most often the result. This is because people prefer the devil they know and are worried about big change. Hence the obvious tactic of No campaigns is to play up the worry. The times when change wins is often when there is an anti-establishment vote (Renwick 2014). This organic rise of self-starting Yes groups not only prefigures a type of politics that reflects a changed society but may also help to create the conditions necessary for a bigger Yes vote. Such an effect may well help to demonstrate the effectiveness of the new forms in connecting with people and in challenging the establishment and so encourage change within the mainstream.

A victory for this type of politics might force a lightening of command and control and the encouragement of more bottom-up political organisation. The Yes fringe is formed into network of coalition with no obvious leader but a shared cause. The Scottish referendum could accelerate the political evolution in Scotland and allow us to lead the way in creating a different politics.

Despite seeing no point at all in voting in any other elections our focus group members were almost all going to vote in the Scottish independence referendum. The two people that said they would not gave reasons of not being Scottish and feeling it was up to Scots to decide. The rest made statements like:

> This is the biggest decision in our lives and I'm taking part.
>
> Dundee group

> This is a real chance of something.
>
> young group

> Once it's done there's no goin back.
>
> Glasgow group

With polls consistently showing a projected high turnout by historic standards this will be the first election for decades when the political biceps of 'missing Scotland' will be flexed. Whether it is a Yes or a No vote this should be a signal to those with authority that when you give people something to vote for, or against, then democracy will work.

A society and politics based on fear and a political class without courage to propose and take forward radical political reform puts our politics at risk and misses out on an opportunity to take democracy forwards in a new and exciting direction. It may be that things have shifted that much that it is no longer up to the elites what happens next. They either help it happen or are pushed out of the way and left behind. If 'missing Scotland' can believe that they matter again, that they can make something change, then it may prove very difficult to get them back on their sofas in which case whatever the outcome in September 2014 Scotland could prove to be a very exciting place to be. Indeed, if people recognise that they have an inherent power and find their collective voice, the independence referendum could be the beginning of much more far-reaching, exciting and unpredictable change which have repercussions and consequences for years to come.

References

Aidan, J and Black, A (2014), Scottish independence: Currency union block could hurt firms, says Alex Salmond. BBC News Website. http://www.bbc.co.uk/news/uk-scotland-scotland-politics-26220638.

Aidan, J and Black, A (2014), Scottish independence: 'Yes' vote means leaving pound, says Osborne. BBC News Website 13 February 2014. http://www.bbc.co.uk/news/uk-scotland-scotland-politics-26166794.

Barker, K (2004), The Review of Housing Supply. London. HM Treasury.

BBC (2013), Waive rights for shares' employment comes into force BBC News Website 1 September 2013. http://www.bbc.co.uk/news/business-23920163.

BBC (2013) Labour Party's Falkirk seat selection row continues. BBC News Website 4 July 2013. http://www.bbc.co.uk/news/uk-scotland-scotlandpolitics-23176525.

Berube, M (1996), 'Public Perceptions of the Universities and Faculty' Academe, 82(4), July-August: 10–17.

Black, A. (2012), Scottish independence: UK consultation supports single question, BBC News Website. http://www.bbc.co.uk/news/uk-scotland-scotland-politics-17600791

Bort, E, McAlpine, R and Morgan, G (2012), *The Silent Crisis, Failure and Revival in Local Democracy in Scotland*. Reid Foundation.

Boyd, S (2013), *Economics of the White Paper* Pt 2: Industrial Strategy. Scottish Trade Union Congress.

Brand, R (2013), Russell Brand on revolution: 'We no longer have the luxury of tradition'. *New Statesman* 24 October 2013. http://www.newstatesman.com/politics/2013/10/russell-brand-on-revolution.

Cable, V (2012), 'Letter on industrial policy in full', *Daily Telegraph*, 6 March 2012.

Cairney, P (2007), 'The Professionalization of MPs: Refining the "Politics-Facilitating" Explanation', *Parliamentary Affairs*, 60 (2), 212–233.

Cairney, P, Keating, M and Wilson, A, *Political Classes in Multi-level Systems: British Legislatures in Comparative Perspectives*, unpublished.

Census 2011: Key Results on Education and Labour Market in Scotland – Release 2B. http://www.nrscotland.gov.uk/news/2013/census-2011-release-2b.

Common Weal (2013), Why we need an industrial policy, Common Weal.

Conservative Party (2013), 'Where we stand' Conservative Party Website. http://www.conservatives.com/policy/where_we_stand/economy.aspx.

Crerar, P (2014), 'London mayor Boris Johnson backs Met in bid for water cannon', *London Evening Standard* 19 March 2014, http://www.standard.co.uk/news/london/london-mayor-boris-johnson-backs-met-in-bid-for-water-cannon-9201618.html.

Curtice, J and Steven, M (2011), Scottish Parliament Election Report 2011. Edinburgh, Electoral Reform Society.

Curtice, J (2012), Scottish Local Government Election Report 2012. Edinburgh, Electoral Reform Society.

Dewey, J (1927), *The Public and Its Problems*. New York, Swallow.

Economist Democracy Index 2013, https://portoncv.gov.cv/dhub/porton.por_global.open_file?p_doc_id=1034

Economist Explains: How North Korean Elections Work, 5 March 2014.

Engels, F and Marx, K (1847), *The Poverty of Philosophy*, Paris.

Escobar, O (2013), Extracted from response to the Scottish Government's Community Empowerment Bill consultation.

Fischer, F (2009), *Democracy and Expertise*. Oxford, Oxford University Press

Ford, R and Goodwin, M (2014), *Revolt on the Right: Explaining Support for the Radical Right in Britain*, London, Routledge.

Freedman, L (2013), *Strategy: A History*, Oxford, Oxford University Press.

Fukuyama, F (1989), *The End of History*, National Interest (16): 3–18.

Gramsci, A (1929), Letter from Prison, 19 December 1929.

Gould, R (2007), Scottish elections 2007: The independent review of the Scottish Parliamentary and local government elections 3 May 2007. Edinburgh. Electoral Commission.

Hasan, M (2010), 'David Cameron praises the philosophy behind WikiLeaks'. *New Statesman*, 29 November 2010. http://www.newstatesman.com/blogs/mehdi-hasan/2010/11/interesting-quote-david

Hassan, G (2014), *Caledonian Dreaming: The Quest for a Different Scotland*, Edinburgh, Luath Press.

Hassan, G and Shaw, E (2012), The Strange Death of Labour Scotland, Edinburgh, Edinburgh University Press.

Illich, I (1989), *A Celebration of Awareness: A Call for Institutional Revolution*. Garden City, NY, Doubleday.

Jones, O (2013), Workfare: 'Why did so many Labour MPS accept this brutal, unforgivable attack on vulnerable people?' *Independent* 20 March 2013, http://www.independent.co.uk/voices/comment/workfare-why-did-so-many-labour-mps-accept-this-brutal-unforgivable-attack-on-vulnerable-people-8542193.html

Kirkup, J (2009), 'George Osborne: Britain risks Greek tragedy over deficit'. *Telegraph*, 20 December 2009. http://www.telegraph.co.uk/finance/budget/6851915/George-Osborne-Britain-risks-Greek-tragedy-over-deficit.html

Korris, M (2013), *Audit of Political Engagement 10*, London, Hansard Society. http://www.hansardsociety.org.uk/audit-of-political-engagement-10/

Labour Party (2013), *One Nation Economy: Policy Review*, http://www.yourbritain.org.uk/uploads/editor/files/ONE_NATION_ECONOMY.pdf.

Martin, I (2014), 'Ed Miliband's promised break-up of RBS and Lloyds puts Mark Carney on notice'. *Telegraph*, 17 January 2014. http://blogs.telegraph.co.uk/news/iainmartin1/100255229/ed-milibands-promised-break-up-of-rbs-and-lloyds-puts-mark-carney-on-notice/.

Mason, R (2014), 'Lobbying bill passes through House of Lords', *Guardian*, 28 January 2014, http://www.theguardian.com/politics/2014/jan/28/lobbying-bill-passes-house-lords.

Mirrilees, J et al (2011), *Tax by Design: Review of the UK Tax System*, Institute of Fiscal Studies.

Mooney, C (2013), 'Paul Krugman: Austerity Is Not the Answer' Mother Jones. 31 January 2013. http://www.motherjones.com/politics/2013/01/paul-krugman-economics-keynes.

Neate, R (2013), 'Pay workers more, CBI chief tells thriving firms' *Guardian,* 30 December 2013. http://www.theguardian.com/money/2013/dec/30/pay-workers-more-cbi-firms.

Oborne, P (2014), 'Let's support Ed Balls's 50p tax rate instead of George Osborne's shameful attack on the poor', 27 January 2014, *Daily Telegraph.* http://blogs.telegraph.co.uk/news/peteroborne/100256699/lets-support-ed-ballss-50p-tax-rate-instead-of-george-osbornes-shameful-attack-on-the-poor/.

Office for National Statistics (2014), *Measuring National Well-being, Life in the UK, 2014.* ONS.http://www.ons.gov.uk/ons/rel/wellbeing/measuring-national-well-being/life-in-the-uk--2014/index.html.

Pidd, H (2010), 'Tony Blair memoirs: A Journey sparks anger at "self pity and mockery", *Guardian,* 1 September 2010, http://www.theguardian.com/politics/2010/sep/01/tony-blair-memoirs-anger-unions.

Progress (2012), 'Character, not class', 1 November 2012, http://www.progressonline.org.uk/2012/11/01/character-not-class/.

Renwick, A (2014), 'Scotland's independence referendum: do we already know the result?', Our Kingdom, 20 January 2014, http://www.opendemocracy.net/ourkingdom/alan-renwick/scotlands-independence-referendum-do-we-already-know-result

Rigby, E (2013), 'Coalition Urged to stick to Industrial Strategy' *Financial Times.* 11 September 2013.

Runciman, D (2014), *The Confidence Trap.* Princeton University Press.

Schnieder, H (2013), 'An amazing mea culpa from the IMF's chief economist on austerity', *Washington Post,* 3 January 2013, http://www.washingtonpost.com/blogs/wonkblog/wp/2013/01/03/an-amazing-mea-culpa-from-the-imfs-chief-economist-on-austerity/.

Scottish Government (2013), *Rent Services Scotland Statistics.*

Scottish Government (2013), *Scotlands Future White Paper.*

STUC (2014), *A Just Scotland: Second Report,* http://www.ajustscotland.org/files/Report/AJS2 per cent2ofinal.pdf.

Taylor, B (2012), 'Labour's Johann Lamont questions free-for-all policy approach', BBC News Website, 25 September 2012. http://www.bbc.co.uk/news/uk-scotland-scotland-politics-19711805.

Terry, C (2012), *A Review of Electoral Registration*, London, Electoral Reform Society.

The Resolution Foundation (2012), *Gaining from Growth, The Final Report of the Commission on Living Standards*, London, The Resolution Foundation.

Thompson, P (2013), *Analysis of tax and benefit changes in the autumn statement*, London. Institute of Public Policy Research.

UK Government (2014), https://www.gov.uk/government/news/government-delivering-200-employment-tax-cut-per-employee.

UK Government (2014), https://www.gov.uk/vat-rates.

UK Parliament Website (2014), House of Lords Reform. http://www.parliament.uk/about/living-heritage/evolutionof parliament/houseoflords/house-of-lords-reform/overview/hereditarypeersremoved/.

Watson, I (2014), Minimum wage set to become pre-election battleground. BBC News Website, 8 January 2014. http://www.bbc.co.uk/news/uk-politics-25656435.

Wheeler, B (2012), Denis MacShane urges 'all working class' MP short-lists, BBC News Website, http://www.bbc.co.uk/news/uk-politics-18969789.

Wintour, P (2013), 'John Major 'shocked' at privately educated elite's hold on power' Guardian, 11th November 2013. http://www.theguardian.com/politics/2013/nov/11/john-major-shocked-elite-social-mobility.

Workers Liberty (2012), 'How Unite plans to change the Labour Party'. http://www.workersliberty.org/story/2012/07/11/how-unite-plans-change-labour-party.

Some other books published by **LUATH** PRESS

Power Failure

Exploring how Scotland is run and what it
means for our democracy
Robin McAlpine and Will Dinan
ISBN: 978-1-910021-35-4 PBK £7.99

*We may not know exactly
where power is but we
know how to control it.
Choosing not to is not a
neutral act but a validation of
government by cartel. It really
is our choice.*

A select few hold a monopoly of power
over Scotland. But why is this? And what
can be done about it?

In *Power Failure*, Robin McAlpine and Will
Dinan strip back the power dynamics
involved in Scottish politics, examining
the nation's leading political elites,
corporations, policy-makers and pressure
groups, and exploring the social, political
and economic implications. This book is
essential reading if you want to know who
is currently running Scotland, and how
you can take control from them.

Generation Scot Y

Scotland's 20-somethings: a serious
generation for serious times
Kate Higgins
ISBN: 978-1-910021-48-4 PBK £7.99

Born in the 1980s and 1990s
and comprising primarily
of the children of the baby
boomers, Generation Y is
often perceived as being the
generation that wants it all.

Think you know what
makes Scotland's 20-somethings tick?
Knowing who Generation Y in Scotland
– Generation ScotY – is, matters for our
economy, our society and our political
culture.

Generation ScotY has grown up with
devolution: are they ready to embrace full
nationhood? How has Scotland's independence referendum affected them and what
does it mean for their future?

In this book, political blogger at Burdz
Eye View, Kate Higgens explores all this
and more – Generation ScotY's identity,
influences, values, voting behaviours and
aspirations. Far from being frivolous, this
is a serious generation for serious times.

*This book only skims the surface but dip
in and you'll discover something you never
knew – I did and I'm the mother of one. And
ultimately, you'll find that far from wanting
to have it all, they just want a little of all that
we've had.*

KATE HIGGINS

The Glass Half Full: Moving Beyond Scottish Miserabilism

Eleanor Yule and David Manderson

ISBN: 978-1-910021-34-7 PBK £7.99

A self-help book for the Scottish psyche

Cultural Miserablism: the power of the negative story with no redemption and no escape, that wallows in its own bleakness.

Scotland is a small and immensely creative country. The role of the arts and culture is one that many are rightly proud of. But do we portray Scotland in the light we should?

There is a tendency in film, literature and other cultural output to portray the negative aspects of Scottish life. In Seeing Ourselves, filmmaker Eleanor Yule and academic David Manderson explore the origins of this bleak take on Scottish life, its literary and cultural expressions, and how this phenomenon in film has risen to the level of a genre which audiences both domestic and international see as a recognisable story of contemporary Scotland.

What does miserablism tell us about ourselves? When did we become cultural victims? Is it time we move away from an image of Scotland that constantly casts itself as the poor relation?

From the Trainspotting to the Kailyard, Seeing Ourselves confronts the negative Scotland we portray not only to the world but, most importantly, ourselves.

Do [they] accurately reflect the reality of life in Scotland for the majority of the population or are they just 'stories' we like to tell ourselves about ourselves?

ELEANOR YULE

Our greatest export is the diversity of our fiction, the myriad of alternatives between its contrasts and all its new heroes and heroines. It's time we knew it.

DAVID MANDERSON

Caledonian Dreaming: The Quest for a Different Scotland

Gerry Hassan

ISBN: 978 1 910021 32 3 PBK £11.99

Caledonian Dreaming: The Quest for a Different Scotland offers a penetrating and original way forward for Scotland beyond the current independence debate. It identifies the myths of modern Scotland, describes what they say and why they need to be seen as myths. Hassan argues that Scotland is already changing, as traditional institutions and power decline and new forces emerge, and outlines a prospectus for Scotland to become more democratic and to embrace radical and far-reaching change.

Hassan drills down to deeper reasons why the many dysfunctions of British democracy could dog an independent Scotland too. With a non-partisan but beady eye on society both sides of the border, in this clever book here are tougher questions to consider than a mere Yes/No.

POLLY TOYNBEE, writer and journalist, The Guardian

A brilliant book unpacking the political narratives that have shaped modern Scotland in order to create a space to imagine anew. A book about Scotland important to anyone, anywhere, dreaming a new world.

STEPHEN DUNCOMBE, author

There could be no better harbinger of [...] possibilities than this bracing, searching, discomfiting and ultimately exhilarating book.

FINTAN O'TOOLE

Details of these and other books published by Luath Press can be found at:

www.luath.co.uk

Luath Press Limited

committed to publishing well written books worth reading

LUATH PRESS takes its name from Robert Burns, whose little collie Luath (*Gael.*, swift or nimble) tripped up Jean Armour at a wedding and gave him the chance to speak to the woman who was to be his wife and the abiding love of his life. Burns called one of 'The Twa Dogs' Luath after Cuchullin's hunting dog in Ossian's *Fingal*. Luath Press was established in 1981 in the heart of Burns country, and now resides a few steps up the road from Burns' first lodgings on Edinburgh's Royal Mile.

Luath offers you distinctive writing with a hint of unexpected pleasures.

Most bookshops in the UK, the US, Canada, Australia, New Zealand and parts of Europe either carry our books in stock or can order them for you. To order direct from us, please send a £sterling cheque, postal order, international money order or your credit card details (number, address of cardholder and expiry date) to us at the address below. Please add post and packing as follows: UK – £1.00 per delivery address; overseas surface mail – £2.50 per delivery address; overseas airmail – £3.50 for the first book to each delivery address, plus £1.00 for each additional book by airmail to the same address. If your order is a gift, we will happily enclose your card or message at no extra charge.

Luath Press Limited
543/2 Castlehill
The Royal Mile
Edinburgh EH1 2ND
Scotland
Telephone: 0131 225 4326 (24 hours)
Fax: 0131 225 4324
email: sales@luath.co.uk
Website: www.luath.co.uk

Printed by RR Donnelley at Glasgow, UK